BRAIDING

MANES AND TAILS

BRAIDING
MANES AND TAILS

A VISUAL GUIDE TO 30 BASIC BRAIDS ❖ BY CHARNI LEWIS

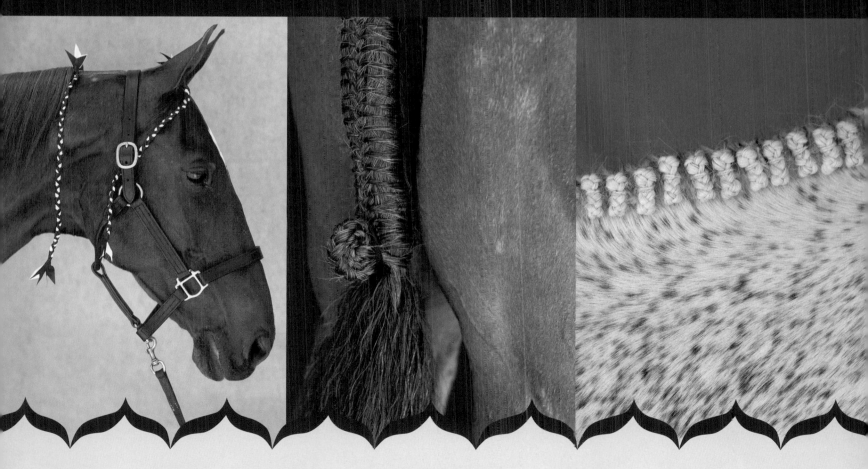

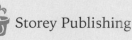 Storey Publishing

CONTENTS

MAINTENANCE BRAIDS

ENGLISH HUNTER BRAIDS

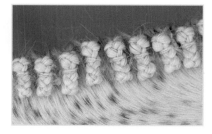
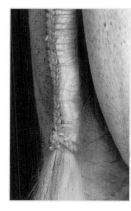
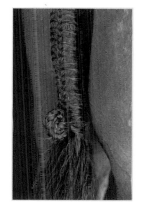
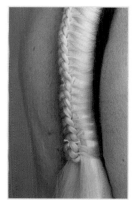

EVENTING KNOTS

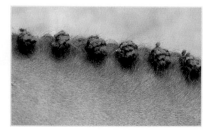
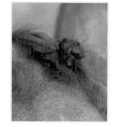

DRESSAGE BRAIDS

Banded Mane and Forelock Loops, *78*

Mane and Forelock Buns, *84*

Taped Mane Loops, *91*

French-Braided Mane, *93*

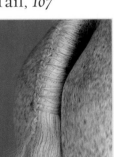

Dutch-Braided Mane, *96*

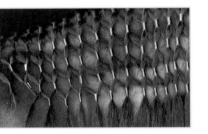

Diamond-Braided Mane, *100*

Dutch-Braided Tail, *103*

French-Braided Tail, *107*

WESTERN MANE BANDING

Mane and Forelock Banding, *112*

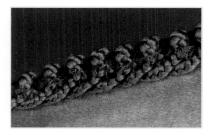

GETTING STARTED

Not only will braiding enhance your horse's beauty, but it is also a fun and relaxing activity that both of you can enjoy. For your horse it feels like a scalp massage. You can turn it into an extension of your grooming ritual: the time and attention braiding requires can result in a bonding experience for you and your horse.

Braids were originally developed for practical reasons, such as keeping the mane from getting tangled in the reins. Later they were appreciated as decoration and as a status symbol, as with the braided horses in the working draft-horse hitches, whose owners had to impress customers and surpass rival companies' hitches. Beautiful braids demonstrate an owner's pride in the presentation and care of her horse.

Always practice safety when working around horses. Braiding manes usually requires clambering on stools, and braiding tails entails standing behind horses. Proceed cautiously, especially at first, and start with a trustworthy horse.

BRAIDING TOOLS

Most of the tools used for braiding are simple items you can find at your tack or craft store. A pull-through, for example, can be purchased; you can make one by bending and twisting a thin coat hanger; or you can substitute a rug hook. In addition, you will need a stool that is sturdy enough to hold your weight but light enough to move around easily as needed.

A	SPRAY BOTTLE	*A spray bottle can be used in addition to a sponge to dampen hair, making braiding easier.*
B	SPONGE	*A medium-sized sponge is used for dampening hair to make it easier to braid.*
C	RIBBON	*Regular ribbon is used for Saddlebred and Tennessee Walking Horse braids and the four-strand forelock braid.*
D	HAIR CLIP	*A small hair clip for human hair works well to hold extra hair out of the way while braiding.*
E	THINNING SHEARS	*These shears do not cut every hair but can be used to thin and shorten the mane on a horse that will not tolerate pulling.*
F	RUBBER BANDS	*Small, commercially available rubber bands are used to secure the end of a braid. They are available in a variety of colors to match the color of your horse's hair.*
G	PULL-THROUGH	*This important tool is used to pull the ends of yarn through the braid. One example is created from a twisted wire coat hanger and the other is custom-made from a metal rod.*
H	SCISSORS	*Regular scissors are used for cutting yarn and trimming the ends of the yarn after you tie a braiding square knot.*
I	TAPE	*Commercial braiding tape is used to hold locks of hair together when making the diamond braid.*
J	PULLING COMB	*This comb has short teeth, so it is easy to wrap hairs around it when shortening the mane.*
K	RAZOR COMB	*A razor comb is used for shortening the mane by making blunt cuts in the longest hairs.*
L	COMB	*A standard comb is used for detangling and combing manes and tails.*
M	CLIPPER BLADE	*A clipper blade is used for shortening the mane by cutting the longest hairs instead of pulling them out.*
N	SEAM RIPPER	*A seam ripper is used to cut the yarn that ties up braids (such as hunter braids) so that they can be taken out of the horse's mane or tail.*
O	RUG HOOK	*A rug hook can be used instead of a pull-through to bring the ends of the yarn back through a braid.*
P	YARN	*Regular yarn is used to tie off braids. It can be purchased in a variety of colors to match your horse's mane.*

PREPARING THE HORSE

A clean mane and tail make the best braids. If
the weather allows, wash them before braiding.
If the weather is too cold for washing, make sure
to comb and untangle before you start.

YOU WILL NEED
Shampoo
Sponge and scrubbing mitt
Hose and bucket

TAIL TIPS
*If the tail is exceptionally dirty, use a scrubbing
mitt or curry comb to gently rub the tailbone and
loosen caked-on dirt and old skin. Use plenty of
soapy water. Keep scrubbing the tail with a sponge
and curry comb until you can squeeze soapy water
down the tailbone and the suds are not dirty.*

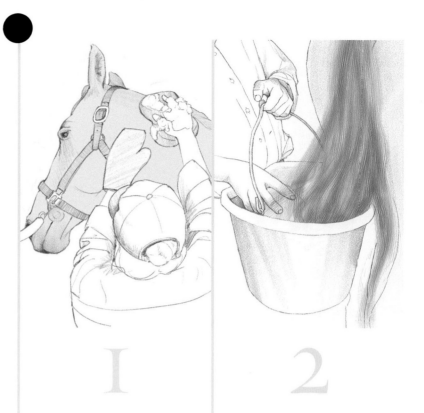

1

Use a soapy sponge
and scrubbing mitt
to work the suds
into the mane and
hair on the horse's
neck. Scrub the
crest of the mane
to clean the roots.

2

Hold the bucket
near the side of the
tail and carefully
dip the long part of
the tail in the soapy
water.

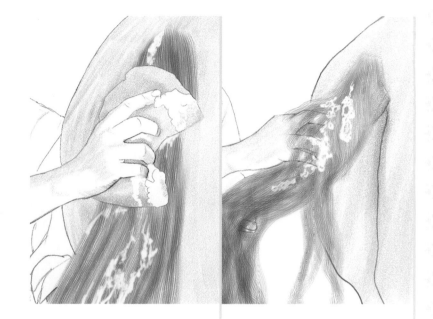

3

Set the bucket aside and use the sponge to spread soapy water on the dock of the tail and along the tailbone.

4

Scrub with your fingertips all along the tailbone, adding more soapy water with the sponge as needed.

Rinse Well

To rinse the horse's mane and tail, use multiple buckets of clean water or a hose and follow the tips and instructions below.

- *Make sure you do not leave any soap in the hair. Dried soap can itch and irritate and cause the horse to rub his tail and body, resulting in hair breakage.*
- *If you use a hose to rinse, spray away from the horse's head and ears, pushing the soap toward his back and down to the ground.*
- *If you use buckets to rinse, dip the long part of the tail in a bucket of clean water and use a sponge to rinse the tailbone thoroughly.*
- *After rinsing, sponge the mane and tail liberally with a solution of 2 cups white vinegar to a bucket of water. You do not need to rinse it out unless your horse has very sensitive skin.*

DETANGLING THE HAIR

If you can't wash the mane and tail, you must still detangle them before you braid.
Hold the tail or a section of mane in one hand and use the other to portion off very
small sections. Starting from the bottom of the tail or mane, comb out one section,
then move to the next, and so on.

HAIR POLISH
*With a badly matted tail you may wish to use a silicone hair polish, confining it to the
long hairs only. Do not apply hair polish routinely, however; it will make the hair
slippery and hard to braid.*

TIP FOR SUCCESS

*If the tail is badly matted, hold it in one hand and pick
out a few individual hairs at a time, separating them
from any tangles and the remainder of the tail. Repeat
with just a few hairs at a time until you have detangled
the entire tail. This technique will also preserve long
tail hairs that can be broken by combing.*

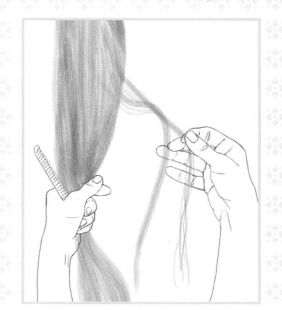

SAFETY WHILE BRAIDING

The ideal space for braiding has excellent overhead lighting, a secure place to tie, and enough room to work around the horse on all sides. A quiet place that is free from distraction helps to keep your horse calm and standing still. When braiding your horse for the first time, use extreme caution. Horses can become startled or irritated and react violently, so it is essential to have sufficient room to move away.

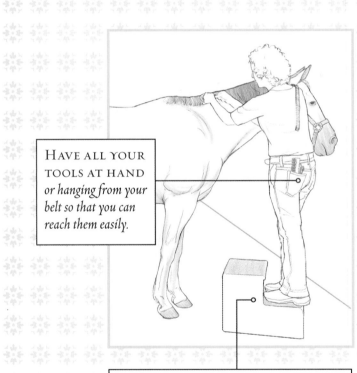

HAVE ALL YOUR TOOLS AT HAND *or hanging from your belt so that you can reach them easily.*

WHEN STANDING ON THE STOOL, *use extra caution not to scare the horse. Speak softly and touch him gently as you climb on, and reassure him again while you step down.*

SAFETY REMINDERS

* *Practice climbing up and standing on the stool a few times before attempting to braid if your horse is new to it.*

* *Make sure that the legs of your stool do not extend under the body of the horse.*

* *Braid only for short intervals as you are learning to make sure the horse does not become restless.*

* *Try not to start braiding around feeding time. Your horse may be impatient if he thinks he is missing a meal. If you must braid then, safely hang a hay net so your horse can eat while you braid.*

* *When braiding your horse's tail, stand to the side when possible. Stay close to his hind legs, with room to move away.*

* *If your horse is tied with a single lead, untie him and put the lead rope over your shoulder before you braid his forelock.*

PULLING A MANE

Short manes are both decorative and functional. Originally manes were shortened so they would not tangle in the reins or fly up in the rider's face when jumping. Since the short mane is easier to comb it can reduce daily maintenance; however, it must be pulled to the desired length about every six weeks. Aesthetically, a pulled mane can improve the look of the horse's neck.

The specific length of the mane may be a matter of personal preference, or it may be dictated by the standards of the riding discipline in which the horse competes. In some English disciplines, the mane must be pulled in order to be braided in the appropriate style for competition.

Use caution when pulling your horse's mane for the first time because some horses will not tolerate it. In such cases, you can try alternative methods of shortening the mane with a clipper blade or thinning shears. Use these carefully to avoid a "cut" look when you are finished.

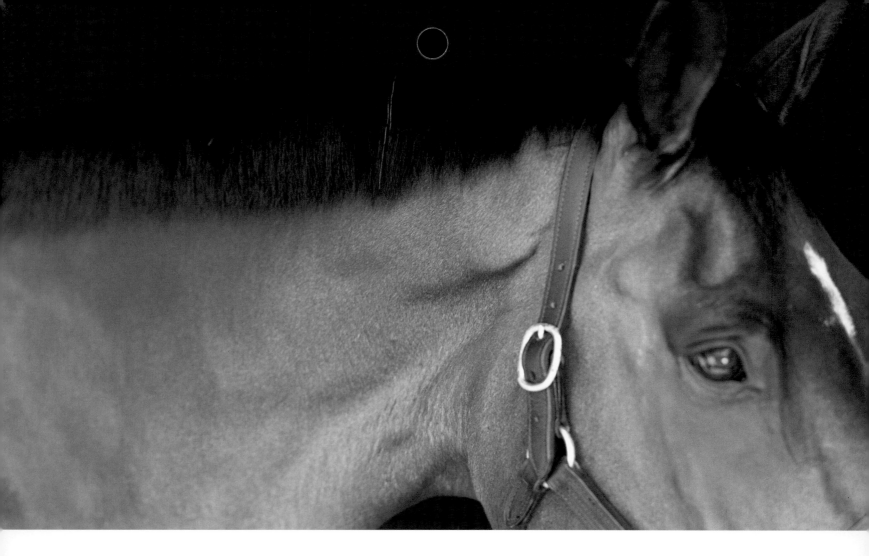

USING A PULLING COMB

Manes are shortened and thinned by pulling out the longest hairs, not by cutting the hair in a sharp line. Most horses do not mind having their manes pulled, but there are alternative techniques for those who do.

YOU WILL NEED

Stool
Pulling comb

TIP FOR SUCCESS

Always pull from the underside of the mane.

SHORT OR LONG?

The typical length for a pulled mane is 3–5 inches (8–13 cm), depending on the shape of the horse's neck and the type of braids you have in mind. If the mane is pulled too short, it will stick up or flip over to the other side of the neck. Manes and tails grow about ½ inch (1 cm) per month.

1 Grasp a small amount of hair and separate out the longest hairs. Back-comb all other hairs toward the crest of the neck.

2 Wrap the longest hairs around the comb.

3 Hold them tightly against the comb while you pull the comb sharply down, removing the hairs by the roots. Repeat until the mane is pulled evenly to the desired length.

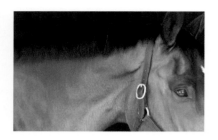

ALTERNATIVE METHODS FOR SHORTENING A MANE

When a horse simply will not let you pull his mane,

here are two other techniques.

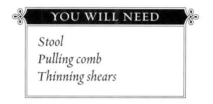

YOU WILL NEED
Stool
Pulling comb
Thinning shears

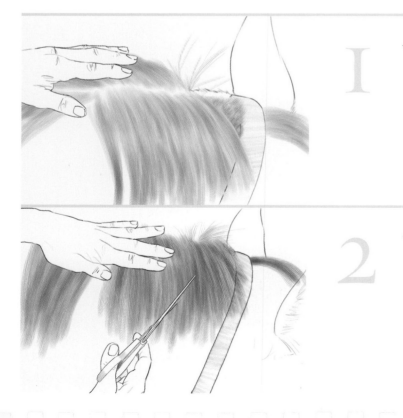

1   With the pulling comb, part a small section of the top of the mane away from the underside. Hold the top portion out of the way.

2   With thinning shears in the other hand, make many small cuts down the hair at a 45-degree angle to the crest of the neck. Then switch to the opposite 45-degree angle and make many small cuts going up the mane.

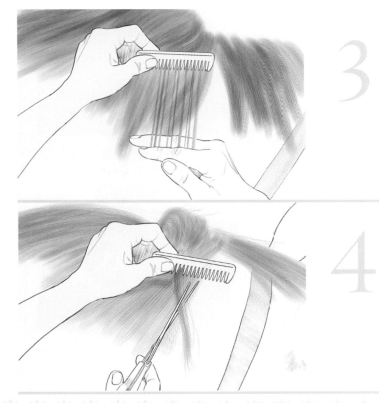

3 Flip the top of the mane back over the shortened portion and use a pulling comb to back-comb a small section of mane. Hold the longest hairs in your fingers.

4 Use the thinning shears at a 45-degree angle to trim the longest hairs first, making several cuts from the crest to the end of the hair, then reverse the direction of the angle and make several more cuts down the length of the hair.

ALTERNATIVE METHOD FOR THIN MANES

When a horse with a thin mane won't let you pull his hair, part a small section of hair on the top away from the underside and back-comb the underside. While holding the longest hairs, use the blade from a large pair of clippers or a razor comb to trim them shorter than your desired length. Then comb down the rest of the mane hairs and shorten those. This method does not thin the mane.

BASIC BRAIDING COMPONENTS

Braids have basic components that, when mastered, can be combined to make a multitude of beautiful effects. At first it will take time and patience to get the hang of braiding manes and tails, but with practice your speed — and the finished product — will improve.

If you are just starting out, begin with the three-strand braid. You can practice with three pieces of ribbon tied to a stationary object like a doorknob. Once you can braid the ribbons easily it is time to try three sections of hair. It is important to keep the strands pulled tightly together in order to make neat braids.

When you are showing your horse, a quality braiding job can distinguish you from the other riders in the ring. It lets the judge know that you are well prepared and that the turnout of your horse is important to you. In fact, if a judge narrows down the choice for the winner of a class to two horses with equally good performances, he or she will usually choose the horse that has the more polished presentation.

THREE-STRAND BRAID

The three-strand braid is the basis for many braiding styles. Once you master it, you will be well on your way to becoming an expert mane and tail braider.

TAIL SAVVY

When working on the tail, do not position yourself directly behind your horse until you know that he is going to stand quietly and be trustworthy.

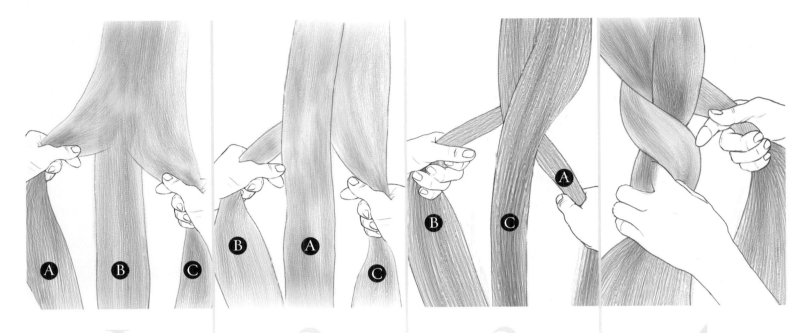

1	2	3	4
Divide your horse's tail hair into three equal parts. Hold section A in your left hand and section C in your right hand; allow section B to hang down.	With your thumb and forefinger, grab section A, cross it over section B, and drop it into the middle. With your left hand, pull section B to the left.	With your right thumb and fore-finger, cross section C over to the middle and drop it. Then with your right hand, pull section A to the right.	Continue to alternate crossing the left and right sections over the middle until you reach the bottom of the braid. Keep the tension even on each section as you work. See pages 33–35 for more on how to finish a braid.

THREE-STRAND
BRAID

TIPS FOR SUCCESS

❧ *Maintain the tension on the sections as you gently stretch them between your alternating hands. Also maintain some tension on the braid from top to bottom.*

❧ *If one of the sections turns out to be smaller and shorter than the others, "borrow" some hair from one of the larger sections by separating a small portion and adding it into the smaller section as the larger crosses over the smaller.*

SIMPLE FORELOCK BRAID

Start a three-strand braid with the long forelock hairs and continue braiding until you need to use yarn or a rubber band to finish, as described on page 34.

The simple forelock braid is described in the chapters on English Hunter Braids (page 57), Eventing Knots (page 74), and Dressage Braids (pages 82 and 89).

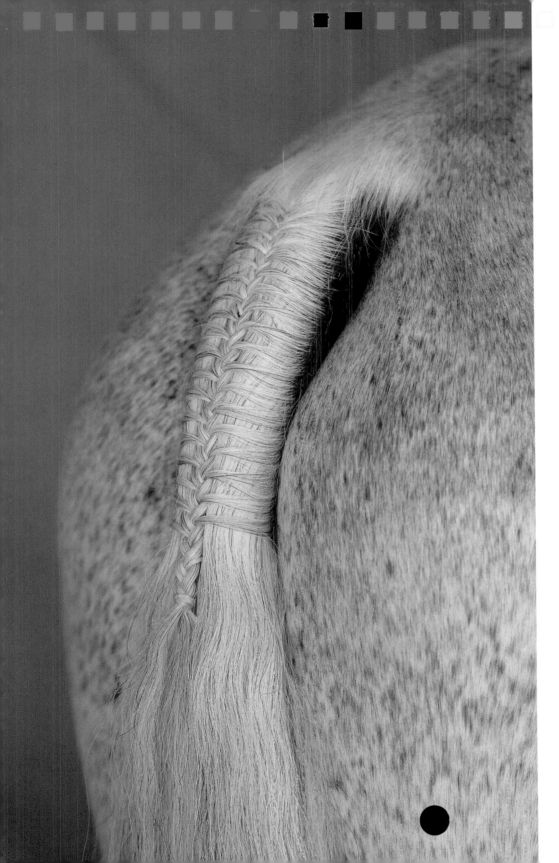

FRENCH BRAID

The French braid is similar to the three-strand braid, but the altered technique creates a unique look. This "overhand" braid is used for English and dressage shows.

YOU WILL NEED

Spray bottle or sponge
Comb
*One rubber band or 2-foot
  (60 cm) length of yarn
  or string*

FRENCH BRAID

1

2

3

PREP WORK
Start with a dampened, combed tail.

At the top of the tail, separate a small portion of tail hair from the left (A) and one from the right (B), then cross the right over the left in the middle of the tail.

Hold these two pieces in your right hand. Take another small portion from the left (C) and cross it over the middle (B) so that there are three pieces.

Twist the right section (A) over the middle (C), so that the right becomes the new middle. Separate another portion from the right (D) and add it to the middle. Pull all braid pieces very tightly.

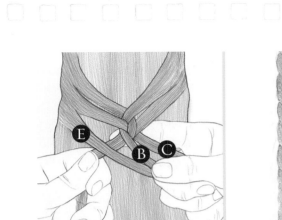

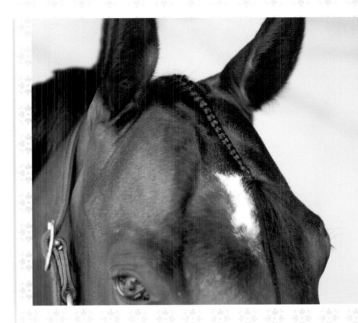

4

Twist the left piece (B) over the middle (A), so that the left becomes the new middle. Add another portion from the left (E) to the middle. Continue braiding, adding hair from alternate sides.

5

About one-third of the way down the tailbone, make a regular three-strand braid with the end hairs from the French braid. Finish with yarn or a rubber band (see pages 33–35).

FRENCH FORELOCK BRAID

Following steps 1–4, French-braid the top of the forelock. Continue adding sections from each side until you reach the end of the scalp.

Use the remaining long hairs to complete a three-strand braid. Braid in yarn and tie off or finish with a rubber band as described on pages 34–35.

The French forelock braid is described in the chapters on English Hunter Braids (page 58), Eventing Knots (page 75), and Dressage Braids (pages 83 and 90).

DUTCH BRAID

The Dutch braid is similar to the French braid, except that it is created "underhand" instead of "overhand." The braid appears to be sitting on top of the hairs, as opposed to being tucked underneath, as with the French-braided tail.

YOU WILL NEED
Spray bottle or sponge *Comb* *One 2-foot (60 cm) length* *   of yarn or string*

TIP FOR SUCCESS

Remember to cross the side section under the middle section BEFORE *you add your new piece of hair to that new middle section.*

PREP WORK

Start with a dampened, combed tail.

1

Separate a small piece of hair (A) from the farthest left side of the top of the tail and cross it under a small piece from the right (B). Take a third piece (C) from the right and cross it under to become the middle piece.

2

Twist the left section (B) underneath the middle section (C), so that it becomes the new middle. Separate a piece of hair from the left (D) and twist it under the left to add it to the new middle section.

3

Twist the right section (A) underneath the middle section (B), so that it becomes the new middle. Separate a piece of hair from the right (E) and twist it under the right to add it to the new middle section.

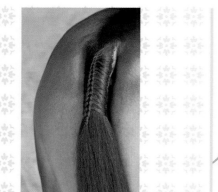

DUTCH BRAID

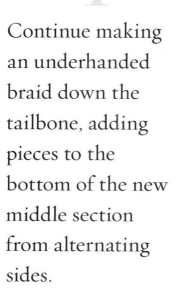

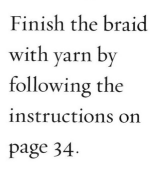

4

Continue making an underhanded braid down the tailbone, adding pieces to the bottom of the new middle section from alternating sides.

5

About one-third of the way down the tailbone, using the end hairs from the Dutch braid, begin an underhanded three-strand braid and continue down the length of the tail.

6

Finish the braid with yarn by following the instructions on page 34.

A finished braid with yarn

Finished braids with rubber bands

FINISHING THE BRAID

There are two ways to secure the end of your braid, whether on the mane or the tail. One is to wind an elastic band around the end of the braid; any rubber band will work, but you can buy small bands that match or contrast with the horse's hair color. The other method is to braid a length of string or yarn into the bottom portion of the braid, then use the end to tie off the braid.

PREPARING THE YARN
To prepare 2-foot (60 cm) lengths of yarn or string ahead of time, hold one end of the yarn in your hand. Wrap the rest around your elbow and up and over your thumb for as many revolutions as you need lengths of yarn, then cut it near your hand.

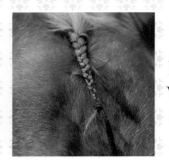

FINISHING WITH YARN OR STRING

TIP FOR SUCCESS

Some braiders prefer to separate both ends of the yarn from the tail hairs and use them both at the same time to tie the knot described below.

I

Begin incorporating the yarn into the side sections when you are 2–3 inches (5–8 cm) away from the desired end.

Fold the yarn in half and place the fold behind the last two turns you made in the braid. Add one end of the yarn to the left section of the braid and the other to the right section. Continue braiding, incorporating the string with each turn.

2

Pinch the end of the braid with one hand and use the other to separate one piece of yarn from the hair. Loop the yarn over the top of the braid at a right angle. Pass the loose end of the yarn behind the braid and pull it through the loop in the yarn. Pull the yarn tight so that it creates a knot, similar to a half hitch. Repeat this step to tie a second knot.

FINISHING WITH A RUBBER BAND

I Once you have braided to within 1–2 inches (3–5 cm) of the end of the hair, pinch the braid with the thumb and forefinger.

2 Wrap the rubber band around the bottom of the braid until it is wound tightly around the hair.

TYING A BRAIDING SQUARE KNOT

The braiding square knot is similar to a traditional square knot, with one extra step to ensure that the knot stays tight. Square knots are used when tying braids close to the crest of the neck and when completing some of the tail braids.

YOU WILL NEED

One 2-foot (60 cm) length of yarn or string

TIPS FOR SUCCESS

❧ *You may want to practice with a piece of yarn or string around a pole to get the hang of tying a square knot.*

❧ *To keep the knot from slipping and becoming loose, you can make a second wrap of yarn or string after the initial base knot is started.*

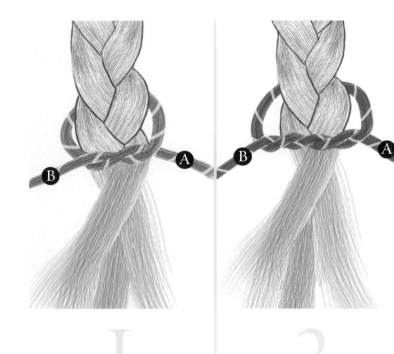
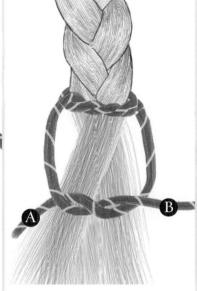

1

Hold one of the two strings, A and B, in each hand. Loosely cross the strings over one another and wrap one end of the string around the other as you would when tying shoelaces. This will make a loop around the braid.

2

Pull the loose end of A through the loop to make a second twist in the knot. Pull the strings to tighten the knot against the pole or braid.

3

Now cross the strings loosely once again with A wrapping first under, then over the top of B.

4

Pull the two loose ends tightly against the pole or braid.

MAINTENANCE BRAIDS

Long manes and tails are beautiful and flow as a graceful horse moves. In some breeds, such as the American Saddlebred, a long tail is the crowning glory of the high-stepping show horse. The long manes of Friesian and Andalusian horses can even reach their knees. These dramatic manes and tails require diligent care and maintenance.

Daily combing and brushing of long manes and tails breaks strands of hair and makes the hair frizzy and unattractive. If you want to keep your horse's mane or tail long, you must conscientiously braid and rebraid the hair every few weeks to let it grow to its maximum length.

Be sure the braids are not too tight if they are to be left in for long periods of time. Otherwise the horse might rub out the hair you have so carefully encouraged to grow.

TRAINING THE MANE TO ONE SIDE

If part of your horse's mane flips over to the other side of his neck, braids can provide a convenient solution. To train the mane to stay on one side (your riding discipline may not care about the side on which the mane falls, as long as it is all on one side), snug braids are put in and left in for several days. For best effect, dampen the mane before braiding.

YOU WILL NEED

Stool
Comb
Spray bottle or sponge
Rubber bands

Tips for Success

❧ Make the braid tight enough to hold the hair down on the neck, but not so tight that the horse becomes irritated and rubs the area.

❧ Leave the braids in for about 10 days.

❧ When you unbraid them, the hairs will be crimped from the braids. Leave these crimps in until they naturally straighten, as they will assist in keeping the hair on the correct side even after the braids are out.

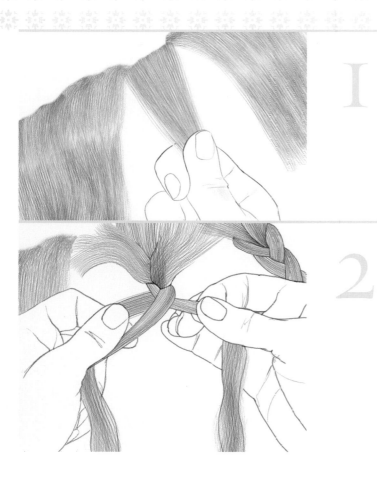

I   Comb the mane to the side of the neck where you want it to lie (the side most of it falls on naturally). Carefully climb up on the stool. With the comb, part off a 2–3-inch (5–8 cm) section of mane that was on the wrong side.

2   Dampen the section of hair, then braid it in a snug three-strand braid. Keep braiding until you have about 1 inch (2½ cm) of hair below the braid, and secure it with a rubber band. Continue parting and braiding, until you have braided the entire section of mane that flips over to the wrong side.

MAINTAINING A LONG MANE

If your horse has an especially long mane, braids can be helpful
in day-to-day maintenance. Make sure they are comfortable for
the long term. Braids of moderate tightness are ideal for
neatening and preserving the mane. If too tight, and left in for
too long, they can cause irritation and become matted.

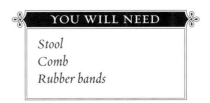

YOU WILL NEED

Stool
Comb
Rubber bands

TIPS FOR SUCCESS

❧ *If you wash your horse's mane, make sure that it is dry before you start braiding.*

❧ *Rebraid every 10–14 days to avoid matting.*

❧ *When braiding at the withers, make sure that the braids are loose enough to allow the horse to lower his head to the ground without pulling out the hairs.*

1 Section off a 2–3-inch (5–8 cm) section of mane near the poll.

2 Braid the section with a three-strand braid that is snug but won't be uncomfortably tight over an extended period of time.

3 Keep braiding until you have about 1 inch (2½ cm) of hair left, and then fasten with a rubber band. Repeat down the neck to the withers. If the mane is shorter there, you may want to leave it unbraided.

PRESERVING
A LONG TAIL

If you want your horse's tail to grow to its full potential length, a braid can protect the hairs from breakage due to tangles, snags, or frequent brushing.

YOU WILL NEED

Two 2-foot-long (60 cm) shoelaces or other long, thin pieces of cloth
One discarded clean sock or commercial tail bag

TAIL BAGS

You can use a commercial tail bag with a Velcro closure to cover and protect the braid. Slip the tail into the bag and push the Velcro strap between the hairs above the tied braid, securing the strap to the other side of the tail bag. The bag will help keep the tail clean and protect it from getting snagged.

Use caution, however, the first few times you use it. If the horse is not accustomed to it, he may be frightened by his own tail.

You can also use commercial veterinary wrap — which sticks to itself but is nonadhesive — to cover the tail instead of using a sock or tail bag.

TIPS FOR SUCCESS

❧ *Stand to the side of your horse as you braid his tail.*

❧ *Divide the tail hairs into three even sections below the tailbone.*

❧ *Rebraid the tail every 2 to 3 weeks to prevent it from matting.*

PREP WORK

Before you begin, make sure all of the tail hairs are detangled. This is one time you may wish to use a silicone hair polish to detangle the tail. (See page 14 for information on detangling.)

1

Start a three-strand braid (pages 24–26) about 3 inches (7 ½ cm) below the end of the tailbone, but do not pull it too tightly at the top. Continue braiding until you are about 6 inches (15 cm) from the end.

2

Fold the shoelace in half and use it to finish the braid as described on page 34.

3

Loop the braid up onto itself. Push the end through the top of the braid, below the tailbone, and pull it out from the back. You should have a 6–8-inch (15–20 cm) loop of braid, with the loose end hanging behind.

PRESERVING A LONG TAIL

4

If the tail is very long, you may have to loop it a second time before you tie it with the shoelace. Make sure that the loops of braided tail are several inches below the tailbone.

5

Use the ends of the shoelace to tie the loose end of the tail hairs around the loop in a braiding square knot.

6

Slide the looped, tied tail into the clean sock so that the top edge of the sock is above the top of the braid but below the tailbone. Use the second shoelace to tie the sock above the braid, but below the tailbone.

MUD KNOT

This braid will keep the tail hairs clean and out of the way in muddy conditions. It is also used for polo ponies, whose tails must be contained so that they do not get caught in the polo mallet. You will secure this braid without the use of string or rubber bands.

TAKING-OUT TIME

Do not leave this braid in overnight, as the tight braids will become uncomfortable against the tailbone. To take it out, simply slide the folded end of the tail out from underneath the strand that has been wrapped around it near the tailbone, and unwind the strand of hair from around the folded end of the tail. Then unbraid as usual.

I

French-braid (pages 27–29) the top of the tail using ¾-inch (2 cm) sections of hair from both sides of the tail. Continue the French braid down to 2 inches (5 cm) above the bottom of the tailbone.

2

Pull out a small strand of hair about ½ inch (1 cm) wide to the right side of the tail. Let this strand hang down outside of the braid, and continue with the French braid to the bottom of the tailbone.

3

At the end of the tailbone, divide the remaining tail hair into three sections and add them to the three sections from the French braid. Now create a three-strand braid to the end of the tail. Keep the extra strand loose.

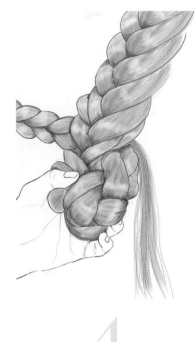

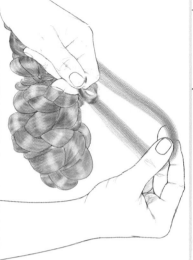

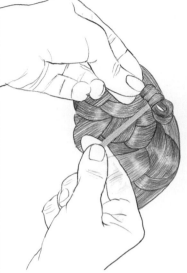

4

Turn the three-strand braid up and wind it snugly around the bottom of the tailbone counterclockwise, with the long extra strand still free. Wind the braid until the end is next to the tailbone.

5

Fold the end of the braid over on itself. Hold the folded hairs in one hand.

6

With your other hand, take the loose end of the hanging strand and wrap it tightly around the folded piece of hair.

7

Keep wrapping it around the folded hair until you have almost run out of room against the tail. Tuck the folded end of the braid under the last part of the wrapping strand to secure the braid.

ENGLISH HUNTER BRAIDS

Hunter braids complement good conformation. Mane braids accentuate the line of a horse's neck and the tail braid shows off the horse's haunches.

This type of braiding may have originated with the sport of fox hunting, where it was essential to keep the horses' manes out of the way of the reins and out of the riders' faces. Because only Thoroughbred horses on the hunt were braided, and other breeds were not, braids (or "plaits") became a symbol of status and quality.

In the past it was customary to create 11 braids, including the forelock braid, if a gentleman was riding the horse and 13 braids if a lady was riding. Today the typical show hunter has an average of 36 to 40 braids in his mane and 1 in the forelock. The shape of your horse's neck will determine how many braids show him off to his best advantage. The more small tight braids you create, the longer and more graceful the neck will appear. If your horse's neck is naturally long, however, you may want to opt for fewer braids.

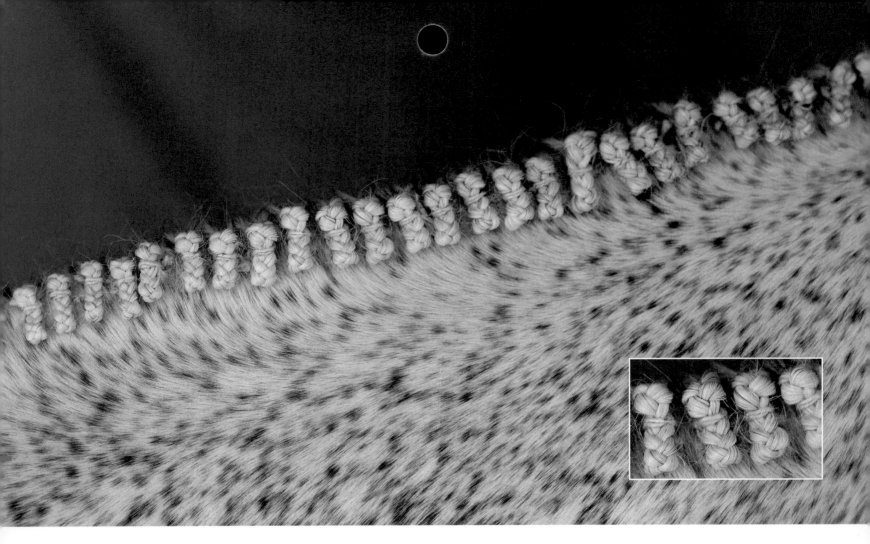

HUNTER BRAIDS FOR THE MANE

Some shows require that the horse have hunter braids in his
mane. These are small, neat loops that are close together
along the crest of the neck. Professional braiders can complete
approximately 36 braids in 45 minutes, but you should allow
more time, at least at first.

Tips for Success

+ *Hang the lengths of yarn through your belt loops or through the ring on the horse's halter so they are easily accessible.*

+ *Count the number of teeth in the comb that you use for the first section of hair and place a piece of tape on the comb at the appropriate spot. This will ensure that the sections are all uniform in size.*

+ *Braids and knots must be neat and tight.*

+ *When unbraiding, use a seam ripper to cut the yarn and the knots.*

Prep Work

It's helpful to have a spray bottle filled with water or commercial braiding spray to keep the hair moist and manageable. If a spray bottle is not available, a damp sponge can be used. Select a yarn color that matches or complements your horse's mane.

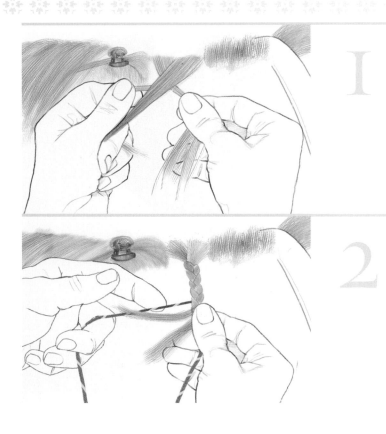

I Start with a dampened mane pulled 3½–4 inches (9–10 cm) long. Use the comb to separate a portion of mane about ¾ inch (2 cm) wide. Use the hair clip to hold the rest of the mane. Start a three-strand braid.

2 Halfway down the braid, insert a piece of yarn to finish the braid as described on page 34.

HUNTER BRAIDS FOR
THE MANE

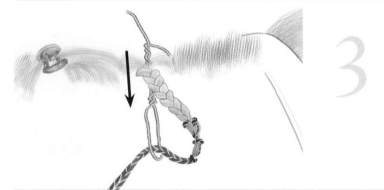

3   Push the pull-through down from the top of the braid next to the crest and feed the loose ends of the yarn through the loop.

4   Pull the pull-through back through the braid along with the two ends of the yarn.

5   Tie the yarn together under the braid in a braiding square knot as described on pages 36–37.

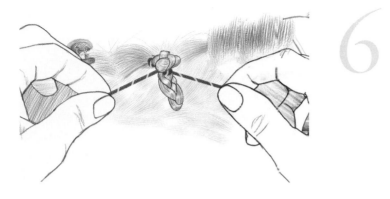

6 Bring the loose ends up to the front of the braid and make a tight braiding square knot parallel to the crest of the neck, so that a small bump forms near the crest. Use scissors to trim extra yarn. Repeat these steps for the entire length of the neck.

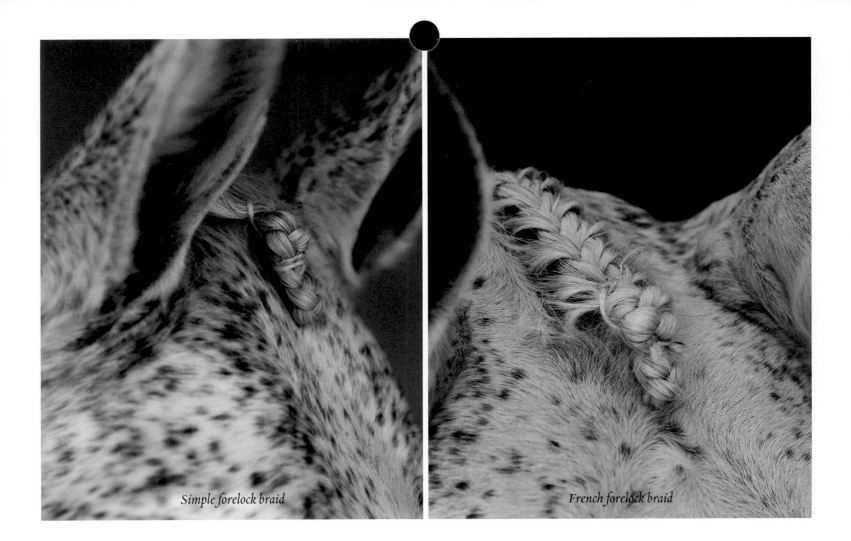

Simple forelock braid

French forelock braid

HUNTER FORELOCK BRAIDS

These braids are left in overnight, so be sure to make them
tight. The hunter forelock braid is tied in the same way as
the hunter mane braid.

❧ **YOU WILL NEED** ❧

Stool
Spray bottle or sponge
One 2-foot (60 cm) length
  of yarn or string
Pull-through
Scissors

SIMPLE FORELOCK BRAID

PREP WORK

Dampen the forelock with a spray bottle or a sponge before proceeding. Use caution when spraying the forelock, as it can startle the horse.

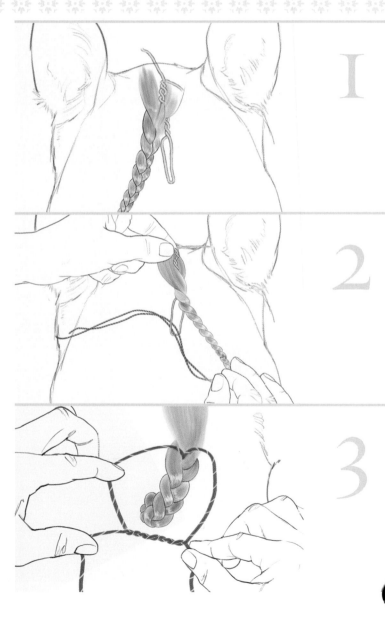

1 Create a three-strand braid finished with yarn, as described on page 34. Push the pull-through down through the top of the braid as high up and close to the skin as possible.

2 Feed the two ends of the yarn through the loop and pull up the pull-through, bringing the yarn with it.

3 Separate the ends of the yarn and bring them down under the braid, one on each side, and tie a tight braiding square knot (see pages 36–37).

SIMPLE FORELOCK
BRAID

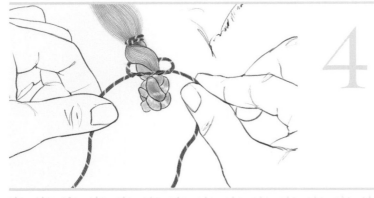

4 Bring the two ends of the yarn to the front of the braid, one on each side, and tie them with a braiding square knot that holds the braid close to the forehead. Use scissors to cut off the tails of the yarn.

FRENCH FORELOCK BRAID
Create a French braid finished with yarn as described on pages 27–29. Push the pull-through down through the second turn of the braid, close to the forehead. Follow steps 2–4 of the simple forelock braid.

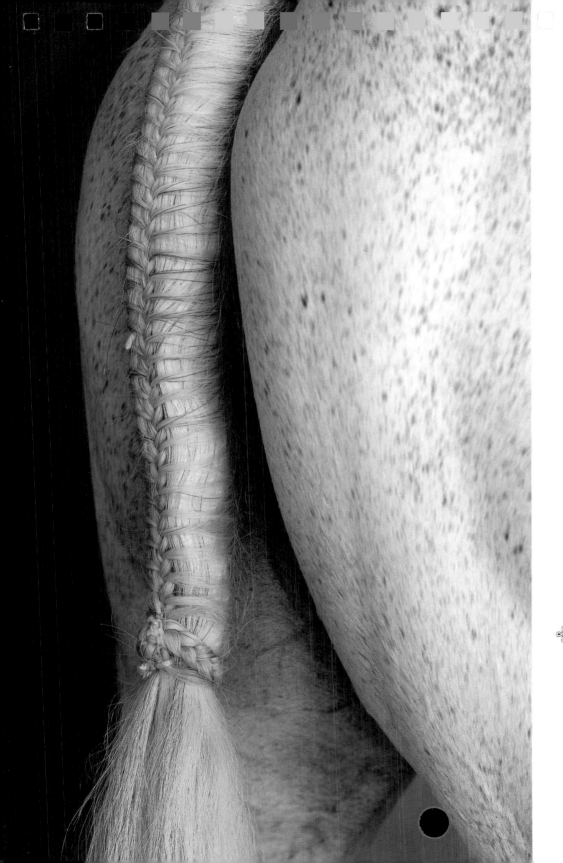

FRENCH-BRAIDED TAIL WITH WRAP FINISH

The French-braided tail accentuates the fullness of the hindquarters and is a nice finishing touch to the show horse with a braided mane. Do this only on a trustworthy horse that will allow you to stand close behind him. Begin by combing out and dampening the tail hairs, especially the ones at the top and sides of the tail.

YOU WILL NEED

Comb
Spray bottle or sponge
One 2-foot (60 cm) length
of yarn or string
Pull-through
Scissors

FRENCH-BRAIDED
TAIL WITH WRAP
FINISH

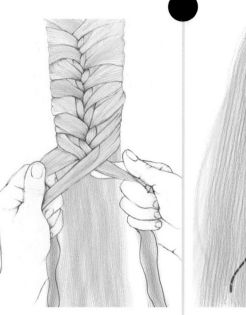

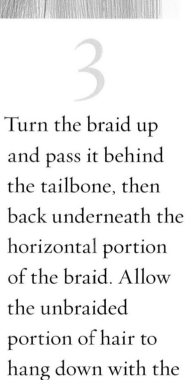

I

Start a French
braid (see pages
27–29) using very
small pieces of hair
from both sides of
the tail. Continue
braiding and
adding hair from
alternate sides
until you are about
three-quarters of
the way down the
tailbone.

2

Braid a regular
three-strand braid
just long enough to
wrap around
the tailbone and
fasten it with yarn
as described on
page 34.

3

Turn the braid up
and pass it behind
the tailbone, then
back underneath the
horizontal portion
of the braid. Allow
the unbraided
portion of hair to
hang down with the
rest of the tail hair.

4

Slide the pull-through under the horizontal piece of the braid and the last two turns of the French braid, then pass one loose end of the yarn through the pull-through.

5

Pull the yarn up through the last two turns of the French braid so that there is one piece of yarn above the horizontal portion of the braid and one below it.

6

Tie the loose ends of the yarn in a braiding square knot (see pages 36–37) around the last turns of the French braid and the horizontal portion of the braid. Cut off the ends of the yarn near the knot.

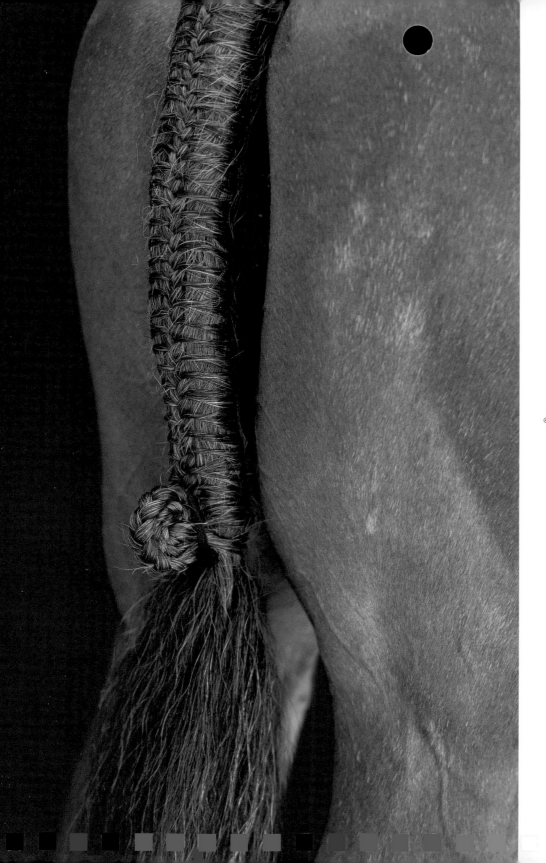

FRENCH-BRAIDED TAIL WITH PINWHEEL FINISH

The pinwheel finish, or snail finish, requires an extra set of hands, but it is an elegant way to decorate a beautiful tail.

YOU WILL NEED

Two 2-foot (60 cm) lengths of yarn or string
Pull-through
Scissors

1

Start by making a French braid down the top three-quarters of the tailbone, then continue with a three-strand braid about 8 inches (20 cm) long, tied with yarn as described on page 34.

2

Fold the braid up on itself, with the loose end pointing toward the braided tail hair. Slip the second piece of yarn through the folded braid loop. The end of the braid must be about 2 inches (5 cm) away from the tailbone.

3

Roll the folded end of the braid tightly, up to the tailbone, so that it looks like a snail shell or a pinwheel, with the extra yarn hanging down from the middle. The loose end of the rolled braid now points toward the tailbone.

4

While you hold the rolled braid, have a helper tie a tight braiding square knot on top of the rolled braid with the hanging ends of the yarn. Roll the tied braid firmly against the French braid with the loose end hanging down.

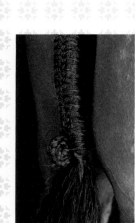

FRENCH-BRAIDED
TAIL WITH
PINWHEEL FINISH

5

Push the pull-through under the French braid at a right angle. Pass the yarn through the pull-through and pull it back through the French braid. Repeat from the other side so that the ends of yarn hang on either side.

6

Pull the ends of the yarn, underneath the French braid, tight to hold the rolled braid firmly against the French braid. Tie a braiding square knot under the rolled braid to secure it firmly against the tailbone.

7

The knot itself will be between the rolled braid and the tailbone. Note that the loose portion of the rolled braid, and the rest of the loose hair, is hanging down. Cut off loose ends of yarn. You can use extra pieces of yarn to secure the roll if it is loose.

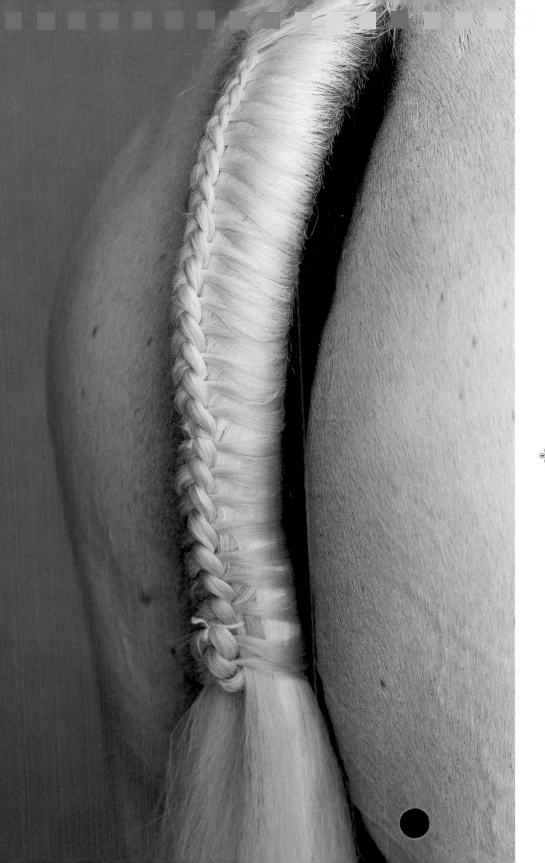

DUTCH-BRAIDED TAIL WITH LOOP FINISH

This beautiful braid is not used as often as the French-braided tail because it has a tendency to pull out the tail hairs if used too frequently.

YOU WILL NEED

Two 2-foot (60 cm) lengths
   of yarn or string
Pull-through
Scissors

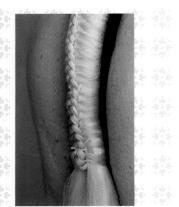

PREP WORK

Create a Dutch braid
(see pages 30–32)
until you are about
three-quarters of the
way down the tail-
bone. Using the ends
of the Dutch braid,
create an under-
handed three-strand
braid that is about
3 inches (8 cm) long,
and finish it with
yarn (see page 34).

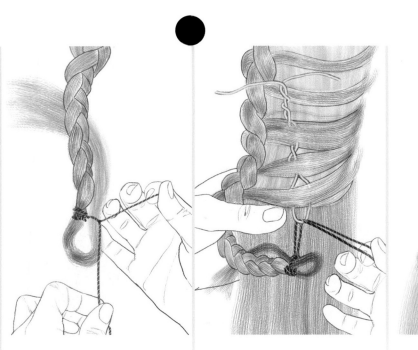

1

Fold the loose
hairs of the braid
so that they are
sticking up parallel
to the braid itself,
forming a small
loop of hair. Tie
a braiding square
knot around the
loose hairs.

2

Push the pull-
through down
through the Dutch
braid about 4 inches
(10 cm) from the
top of the three-
strand braid. Place
the loose ends of
the yarn in the
pull-through.

3

Pull the pull-
through back out of
the braid and draw
up the short portion
of the braid under-
neath the existing
Dutch braid, so that
the three-strand
braid is between the
Dutch braid and the
tailbone.

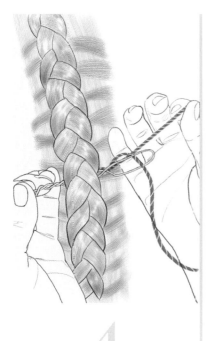

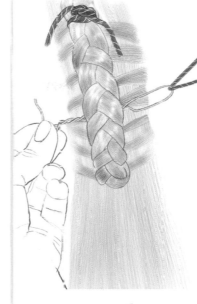
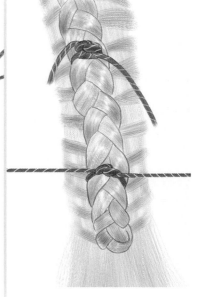

4

Push the pull-through at a right angle under the Dutch braid, directly across from the yarn, and put one of the ends of the yarn through the loop. Pull the pull-through and yarn to the other side of the braid.

5

Tie off the Dutch braid with a braiding square knot (see pages 36–37).

6

Push the pull-through at a right angle under the Dutch braid about 2 inches (5 cm) from the bottom of the braid, and pass one end of the second piece of yarn through the loop.

7

Pull the pull-through back out of the braid so that the yarn is sticking out of either side of the Dutch braid. Tie a square knot at the base of the braid to secure the hair that was pulled up underneath. Cut off loose ends of yarn.

EVENTING KNOTS

In the three-day event the same horse and rider pair must perform a dressage test, complete a cross-country jumping course, and negotiate a stadium jumping course on three consecutive days. In its early years, the sport — named "The Militaire" — was a test of the cavalry horse. The movements in the dressage phase have evolved from strict parade maneuvers that were important training for face-to-face combat.

The dressage phase requires that the horse's mane be braided, but horses can also be braided for stadium jumping. Eventing knots stand away from the horse's neck a little more than hunter mane braids or dressage buns do, but they are formal enough for the dressage court. These knots — or "buttons" — go in more quickly than some of the other types of braids do.

The average number of braids is between 16 and 21, evenly spaced down the horse's neck. This number can vary according to the length of the horse's neck and his conformation.

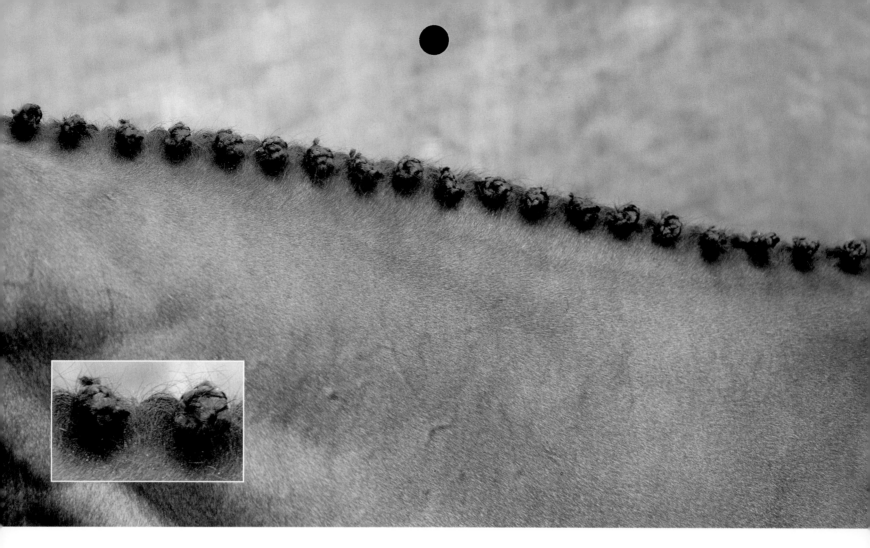

MANE KNOTS

As you create this knot, keep in mind that ultimately there should be 16 to 21 braids evenly spaced down the horse's neck. To begin, pull your horse's mane to 4–4½ inches (10–11 cm).

Starting at the bridle path, part off a section of mane 1½–2 inches (3–5 cm) wide and use the hair clip to hold back the rest of the mane. Start a tight three-strand braid, and tie it with yarn as described on page 34.

Tie the braid in a knot by turning it up on top of itself so that it forms a circle. Bring the loose ends of hair and yarn around behind and then through the opening.

Pull the knot of braided hair tight to the crest of the neck.

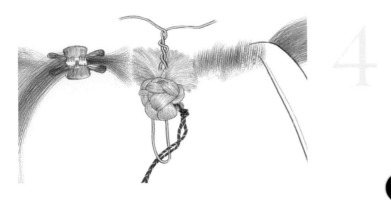

Push the pull-through down from the crest of the neck close to the skin and pass the ends of the yarn through the loop.

MANE KNOTS

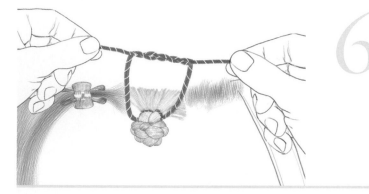

5   Pull the pull-through up through the braid, and the ends of the yarn out the top of the braid. Separate the ends of the yarn and tie a braiding square knot tightly under the braid between the knot and the neck.

6   Tie a braiding square knot on the top of the braid as described on pages 36–37.

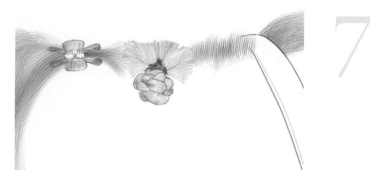

7   Cut the ends of the yarn on either side of the knot near the crest of the neck. Continue down the mane, repeating these steps until you reach the withers.

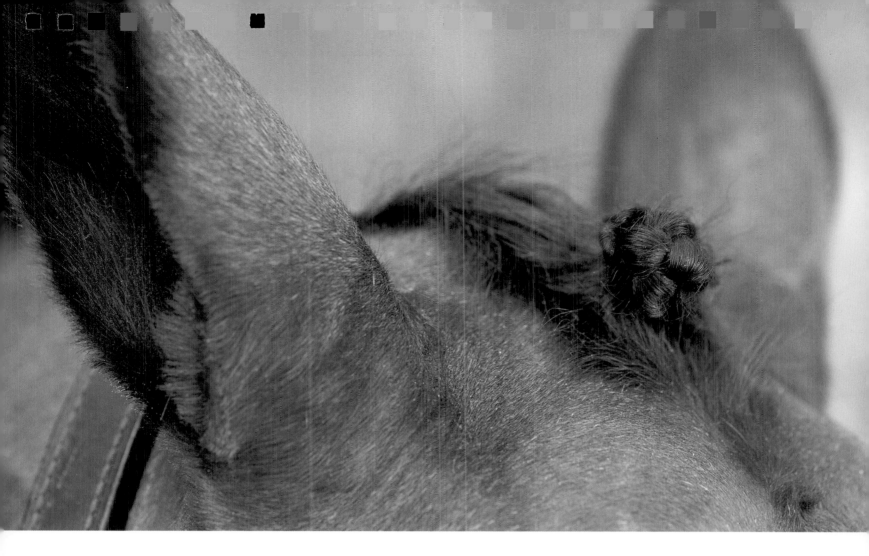

FORELOCK KNOTS

Eventing horses must be braided for dressage. They can be braided for stadium jumping, but they are generally left unbraided for the cross-country phase. You can create the forelock knot with either a simple or a French forelock braid.

SIMPLE FORELOCK KNOT

Prep Work
Start a simple forelock braid finished with yarn as described on page 34.

I   Tie the braid in a knot by turning it up on top of itself so that it forms a circle, with the loose ends parallel to the poll. Push the ends of the yarn through the circle. Pull the knot tightly to the forehead.

2   Push the pull-through down from the top of the braid, close to the skin, and put the ends of the yarn through the loop. Pull the pull-through up through the braid, and the ends of the yarn out the top of the braid.

3   Separate the ends of the yarn and tie a braiding square knot (see pages 36–37) tightly under the braid, between the knot and the forehead.

4 Tie a braiding square knot on top of the braid and cut off the excess yarn on either side of the knot.

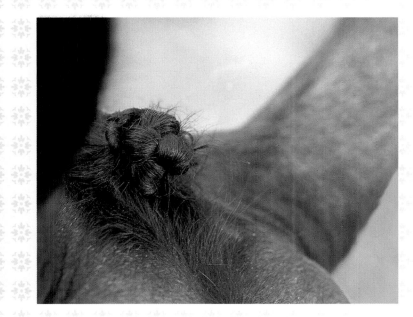

FRENCH FORELOCK KNOT

Start a basic French braid and finish it with yarn as described on page 34. Repeat steps 1–4.

DRESSAGE BRAIDS

The term *dressage* comes from the French word for training, and the specific movements we see in dressage competition today have evolved from exercises developed for the battlefield and parade ground.

Dressage horses are required to be braided for competition. Dressage braids tend to lie down against the horse's neck and, like hunter braids, complement the grace and conformation of the horse's neck. The practice of wrapping the braids with white tape is voluntary, but it draws the judge's eye to the line of the horse's neck and demonstrates the consistency of the horse's outline. Conversely, if your horse is not consistent in his roundness and outline, taped braids will call the judge's attention to this as well.

The average number of braids is between 16 and 21, but there is no exact number specified. An antiquated tradition holds that male horses should have an odd number of braids, including the forelock, and mares an even number, but no one in current competitions adheres to these guidelines.

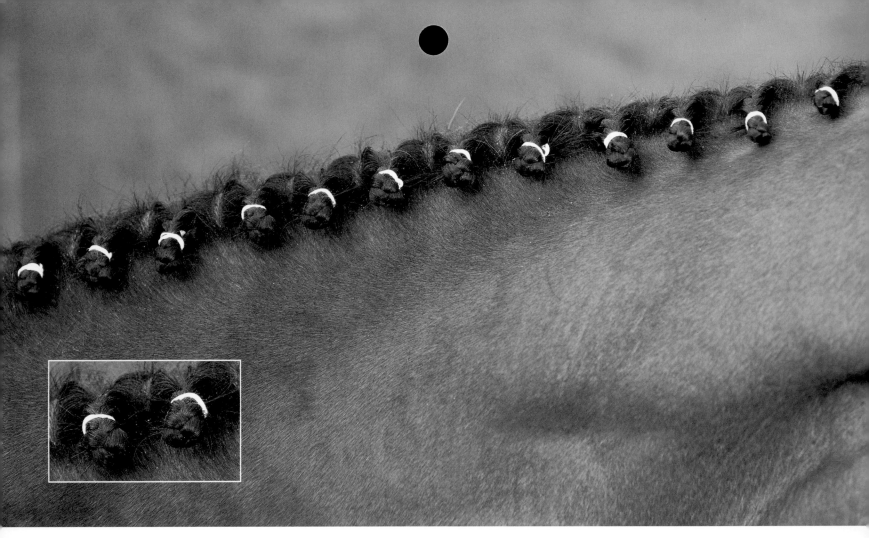

MANE LOOPS WITH RUBBER BANDS

With practice, mane loops with rubber bands can be put in faster than those tied with yarn. However, they usually have to be rebraided daily. They come out much more quickly than braids tied with yarn.

❧ YOU WILL NEED ❧

Stool
Pulling comb
Spray bottle or sponge
Hair clip
Rubber bands

RUBBER BANDS
Braiding rubber bands are commercially available in a variety of colors. Use white rubber bands for a contrasting look, or bands that match the mane for a complementary look.

TIPS FOR SUCCESS

❧ *Keep the rubber bands in a pocket of your pants or your apron so that they are easily accessible.*

❧ *Fold and band the braids as you go, or do all the braids first, then go back and band them.*

PREP WORK

Start with a dampened, combed mane pulled to about 4 inches (10 cm).

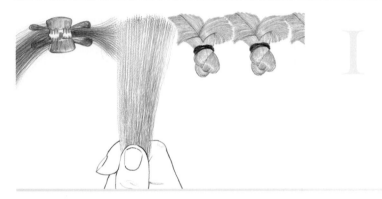

1 Part off a section of mane that is approximately 2½ inches (6 cm) wide, and hold the remaining hair back with a hair clip. Create a three-strand braid that is tight against the crest of the neck.

2 Braid as far down the hair as possible and fold over the ends of the hair before fastening them with a rubber band.

3 Fold the bottom third of the braid up underneath itself.

MANE LOOPS WITH
RUBBER BANDS

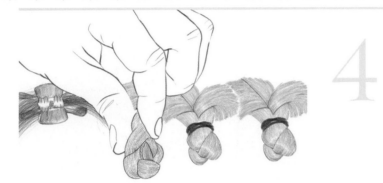

4 Fold the braid under again so that it touches the underside of the braid where it meets the crest of the neck.

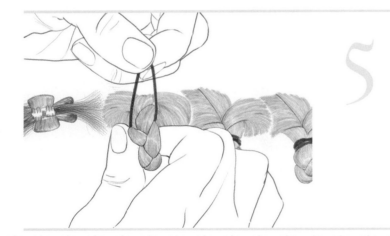

5 Hold this folded loop with one hand as you wind a second rubber band around the folded loop, so that the band is horizontal, or parallel to the crest of the neck. Continue down the mane, braiding and banding until you reach the withers.

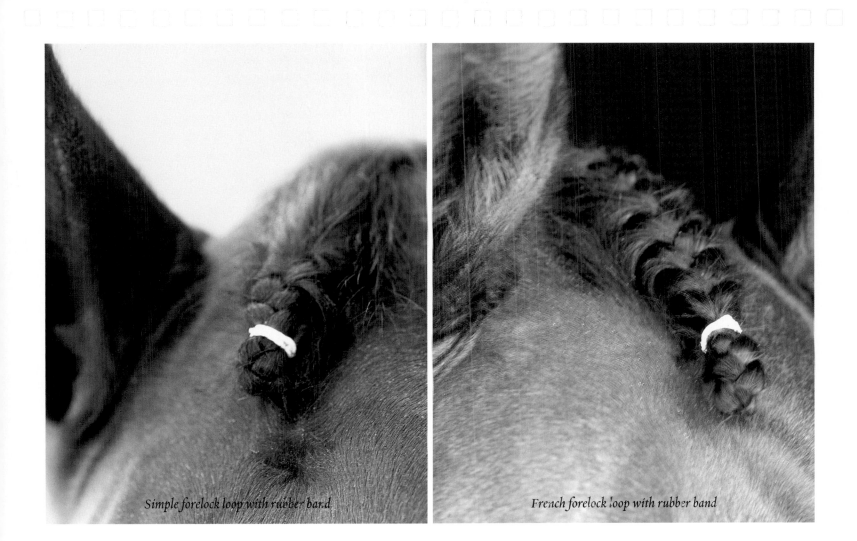

Simple forelock loop with rubber band

French forelock loop with rubber band

FORELOCK LOOPS WITH RUBBER BANDS

This quick, neat braid is one of the easiest to master, but it makes your dressage horse look professionally turned out for the show.

YOU WILL NEED

Stool
Spray bottle or sponge
Comb
Two rubber bands

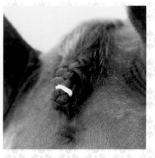

SIMPLE FORELOCK LOOP

PREP WORK
Start with a dampened, combed forelock.

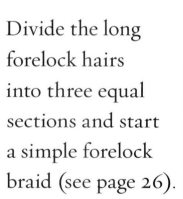

I
Divide the long forelock hairs into three equal sections and start a simple forelock braid (see page 26).

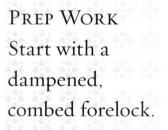

2
Continue braiding as far down the forelock as possible, fold the ends under, and secure with a rubber band.

3
Fold the bottom third of the braid up underneath itself.

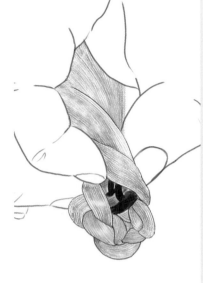

4

Fold the braid under again so that the fold touches the underside of the braid where it meets the forehead.

5

Hold this folded loop with one hand. With the other hand, wind a second rubber band around the folded loop so that the band is horizontal to the poll.

FRENCH FORELOCK LOOP

Start with a dampened, combed forelock, and create a French forelock braid as described on page 58. Follow steps 2–5 of Simple Forelock Loop.

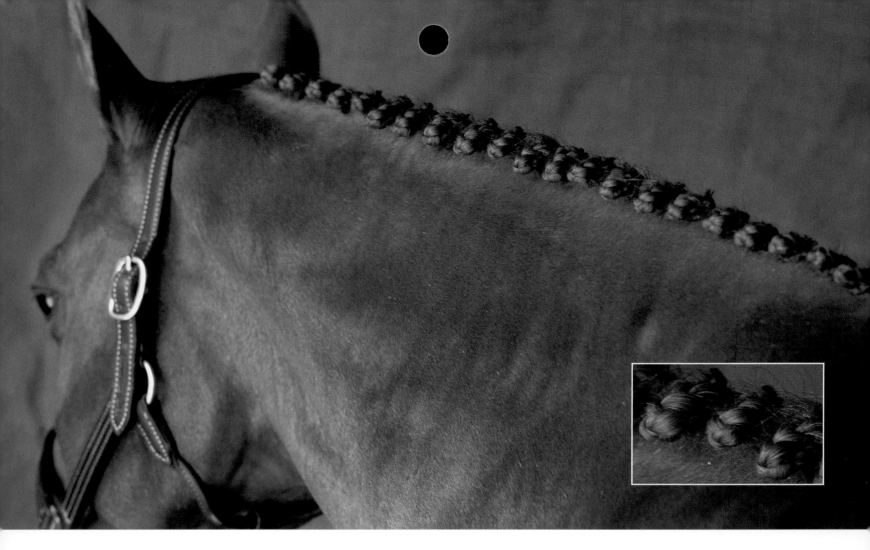

MANE BUNS

This is a convenient mane braid for dressage because the braids lie flat against the horse's neck for a neat look. It is easier if the mane is pulled a little bit longer than for a hunter braid, about 4½ inches (12 cm) in length. As these are dressage braids, you want to end up with between 19 and 21 braids evenly spaced down the neck.

YOU WILL NEED
Stool
Spray bottle or sponge
Comb
Hair clip
25 2-foot (60cm) lengths of yarn or string
Pull-through
Scissors

Prep Work
Start with a dampened, combed mane.

1   Part off a section of mane about 2½ inches (6 cm) in length, and hold the remaining hair back with a hair clip. Start a tight three-strand braid and tie it with yarn as described on page 34.

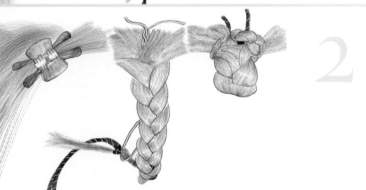

2   Push the pull-through down next to the crest of the neck, and pass the two ends of the yarn through the pull-through.

3   Pull the pull-through with the ends of the yarn and braid back through, so that the braid is sticking up above the crest of the neck.

MANE BUNS

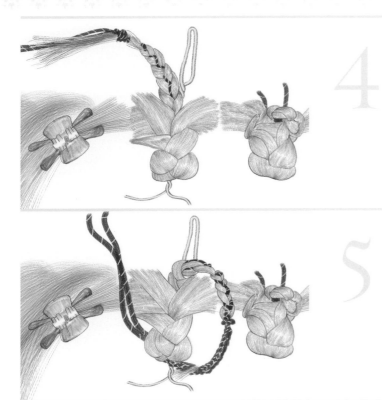

4 Push the pull-through back up through the base of the braid, close to the crest of the neck.

5 Pull the braid up, then wrap it tightly around itself from the right and down under the loop of the braid.

6 Pass the two ends of yarn through the pull-through from back to front.

Pull the ends of the yarn and any remaining braid down through the braid with the pull-through. Keep the tension on the braid.

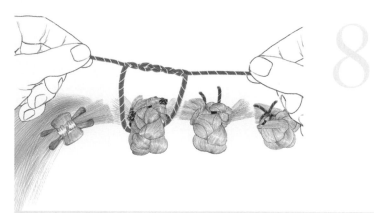

Separate the ends of the yarn and pull them up above the crest of the neck on either side of the braid. Hold the braid down with your thumb as you tie a braiding square knot, so that the braid lies flat against the neck. Cut off excess yarn.

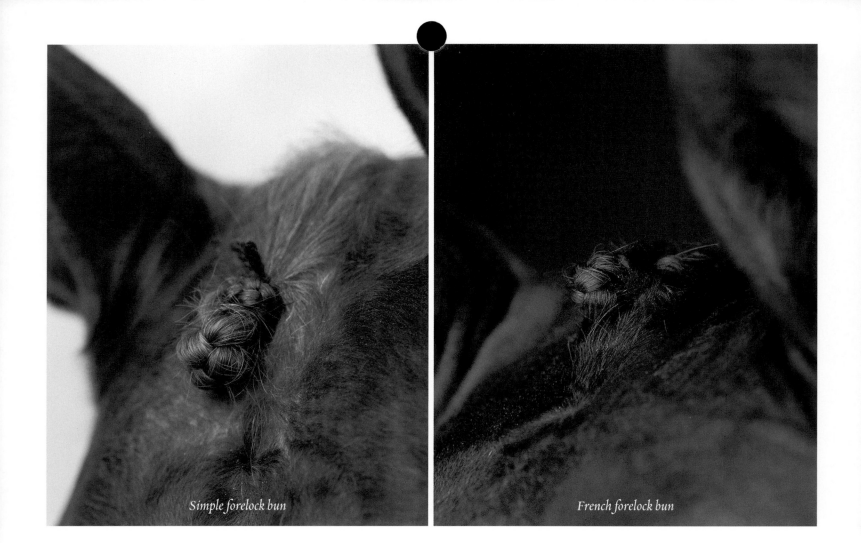

Simple forelock bun

French forelock bun

FORELOCK BUNS

The classy mane and forelock buns last well overnight, so by spending a little more time putting them in, you may be able to save time getting ready later. You can create either a simple or a French forelock bun.

YOU WILL NEED

One 2-foot (60 cm) length
  of yarn or string
Pull-through

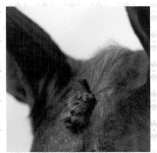

SIMPLE FORELOCK BUN

PREP WORK
Start with a simple forelock braid tied with yarn, as described on page 34.

I
Push the pull-through down next to the scalp at the start of the braid and pass the two ends of the yarn through the pull-through.

2
Pull the pull-through with the ends of the yarn and the braid back through, so that the braid is sticking up above the forelock.

3
Push the pull-through back up through the base of the braid, close to the skin. Pull the braid up, then wrap it tightly around itself from the right and down under the loop of the braid.

SIMPLE FORELOCK BUN

4

Pull the yarn and braid through the pull-through from back to front. Pull the ends of the yarn and any remaining braid down through the braid, keeping the tension on the braid.

5

Separate the ends of the yarn and pull them up above the braid with one end of the yarn on either side. Tie a square knot toward the top of the braid, so that the braid lies flat against the forehead.

FRENCH FORELOCK BUN

Start with the French forelock braid finished with yarn, as described on page 34. Then repeat steps 1–5 of Simple Forelock Bun.

TAPED MANE LOOPS

For a more polished look, and to complement the line of the
neck and highlight the conformation, add white braiding tape
to loops held with rubber bands or mane buns held with yarn.
Tape can also be used to clean up yarn-tied braids that have
been left in overnight and have started to loosen.

TAPED MANE LOOPS

TIME SAVERS

Having a friend cut the tape and hand it to you for each braid will speed up the process. It is also possible to cut several pieces of tape ahead of time and stick them to the cheek piece and ring of the halter so that they are readily available.

I   Cut a length of tape about 2½ inches (6 cm) long. Wrap the tape around the part of the braid that lies flat against the neck. Continue taping in an even line down the neck to the withers.

2   Do not forget to tape the forelock.

FRENCH-BRAIDED MANE, OR RUNNING BRAID

This is a braid for a dressage horse with a long mane. The braid will slip over time, so make it immediately before your class and take it out soon after. This braid is based on an overhand braid with additional pieces of mane added as you work your way to the withers.

```
╔══════════════════════════╗
║      YOU WILL NEED        ║
╠══════════════════════════╣
  Stool
  Spray bottle or sponge
  Comb
  Rubber bands
  Hair gel
```

HAIR GEL
Use hair gel to smooth down any ends that stick up from the crest of the mane.

French-Braided Mane, or Running Braid

Prep Work
Start with a dampened, combed mane.

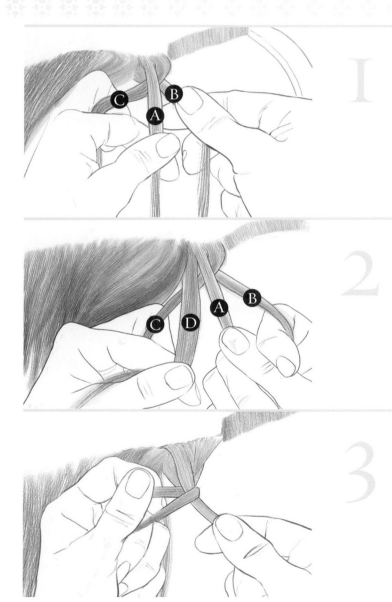

1 Part off a portion of mane about 1–1½ inches (3–4 cm) wide. Separate the hair into three sections and start a three-strand braid. With the first turn, cross section C over section B. Cross section A over section C.

2 Separate another small portion of mane (section D). Add it to section A.

3 Continue braiding for one turn: Cross the right section over the middle (as shown), cross the left section over the new middle, and add hair to the middle section. Keep the braid parallel to the crest.

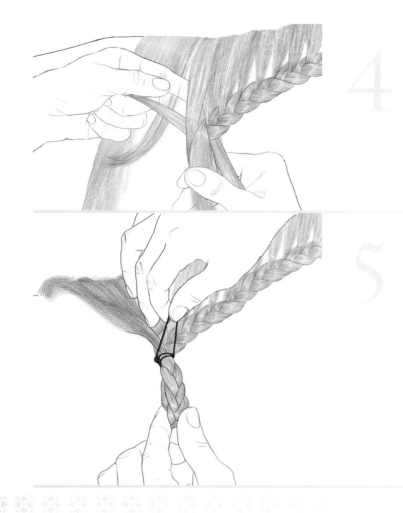

Keep adding hair to the middle section at every other turn of the braid, and continue braiding until you have reached the withers. Then finish with a three-strand braid.

At the end of the braid, fold the remaining hairs over and wind a rubber band tightly around the end, or finish with yarn as described on page 34. Then fold the braid up on itself and use a second rubber band to secure the loop, or finish in a bun as described on pages 84–87.

Finishing the Forelock

With the French braided mane, you can braid the forelock in a loop as described on pages 81–83, and secure the braid with rubber bands. If you choose to create a bun for the forelock, follow the steps on pages 88–90 and secure with yarn.

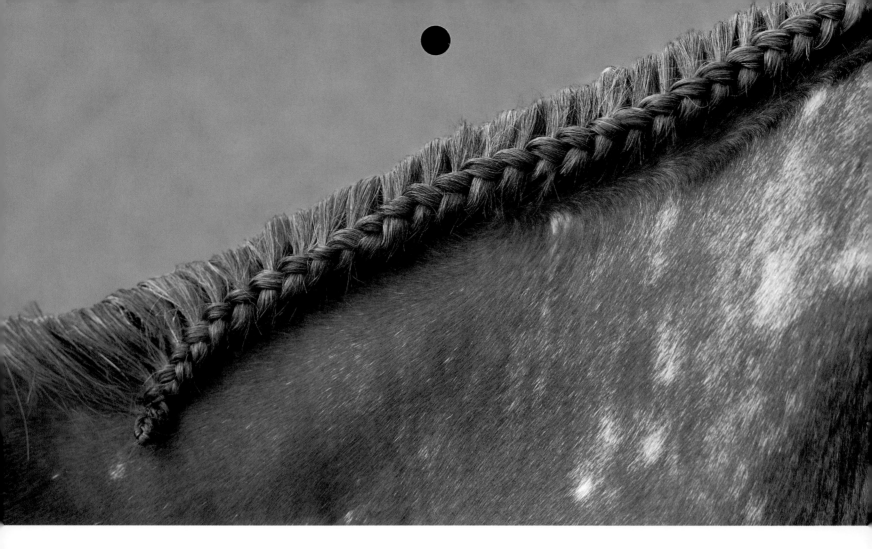

DUTCH-BRAIDED MANE

The Dutch running braid is similar to the French running braid, except that it is braided underhand, pulling the new pieces of mane into the underside of the braid instead of over the top. The braid will appear on top of the mane instead of underneath. (*Note:* The instructions below are for a horse with a mane that hangs on the right side. If your horse's mane falls on the left, use your hands in the opposite sequence.)

HAIR GEL
Use hair gel to smooth down any ends that stick up from the crest of the neck.

Prep Work

Start with a dampened, combed long mane. Portion off a piece about 1½ inches (4 cm) wide near the bridle path or poll and separate into three sections.

1. Start an underhanded three-strand braid. With the first turn, you will bring the right section under the middle section to create a new middle section.

2. Twist the left section under the middle section to create a new middle section.

3. Twist the right section under the middle section to create a new middle section.

DUTCH-BRAIDED MANE

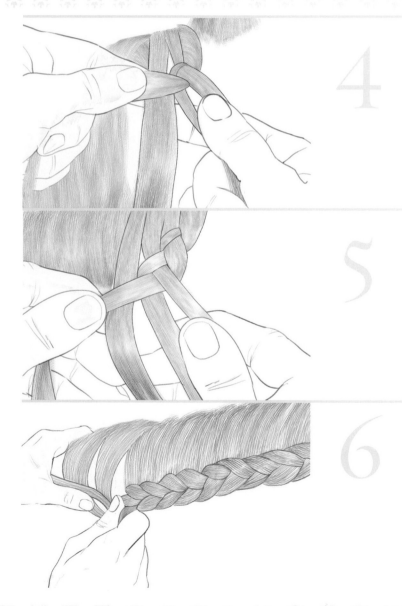

4 As you twist the next left section under the middle section, separate a piece of mane from the left and add it to the middle section, as shown. Twist the right section under the middle to create a new middle.

5 Each time that you twist under the left section, add a portion of mane from the left to the middle.

6 Continue braiding in this underhand manner. Keep the braid parallel to and as close to the crest as possible. When you reach the withers, make an underhand three-strand braid with the remaining hair.

7 Fold the ends of the hair over and fasten with a rubber band, or finish the braid with yarn as described on page 34.

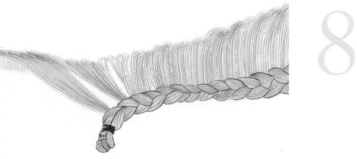

8 Fold up the braid in the same manner that you would for a mane loop (see pages 78–80), and fasten with a second rubber band. Or tie it up as described for making a mane bun (see pages 84–87).

FINISHING THE FORELOCK

With the Dutch running braid, you can braid the forelock in a loop as described on pages 81–83 and secure the braid with rubber bands. If you choose to create a bun for the forelock, use yarn as described on pages 88–90.

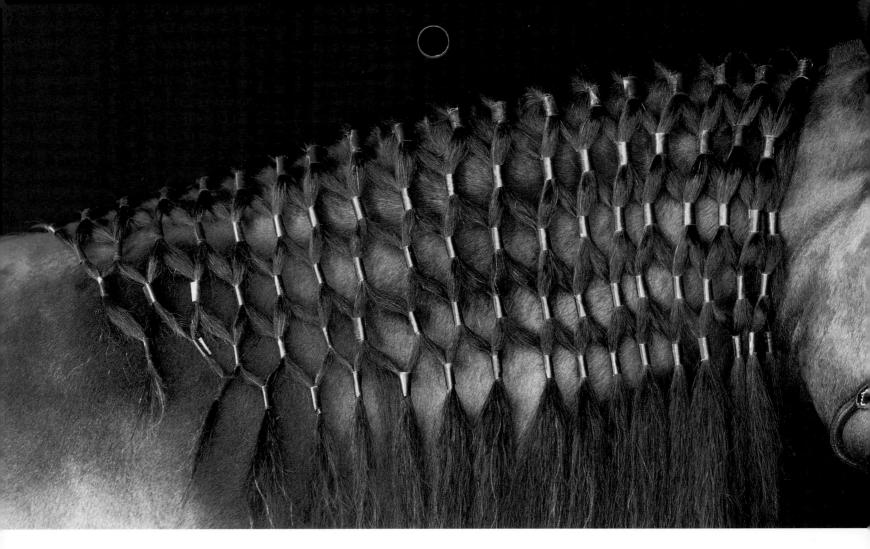

DIAMOND-BRAIDED MANE, OR CONTINENTAL BRAID

This elegant braid is best for a long, thick mane. Although it looks complicated, it is easy to do once you get the hang of it. Do not leave this braid in overnight because the tape can become hard to remove.

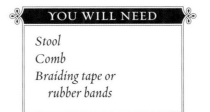

YOU WILL NEED

Stool
Comb
Braiding tape or
  rubber bands

MATCH THE MANE

For a black mane, you can use black electrical tape; for light manes, you can use white athletic tape or commercial braiding tape. Use scissors to cut pieces with even ends.

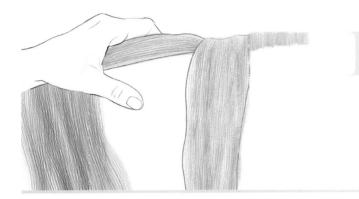

1 Use the comb to separate a portion of mane about 2 inches (5 cm) wide near the poll.

2 Use a piece of tape to gather the hairs together near the crest of the neck or wind a rubber band around that section. Twist the locks of hair together as you tape them to make a tighter bundle.

3 Continue separating out 2-inch (5 cm) sections of hair and banding or taping them until you reach the withers, then return to the head.

4 Part each lock in half and connect the two nearest sections about 3 inches (8 cm) down with tape or a rubber band.

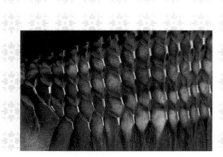

DIAMOND-BRAIDED MANE,
or CONTINENTAL BRAID

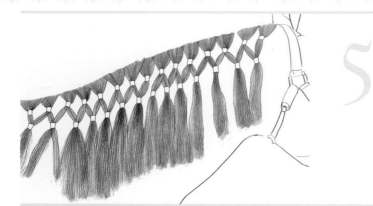

5   Continue parting sections in half and connecting those nearest each other, all the way to the withers, with tape or rubber bands.

6   Return to the horse's head and part each lock of hair in half, and connect each half lock to the nearest half with tape or a rubber band in a straight line.

7   Repeat the process of parting and connecting the sections nearest to each other, all the way to the withers, with tape or rubber bands in a line parallel to the crest. You should have 3–5 rows of tape.

DUTCH-BRAIDED TAIL FOR HORSES WITH LONG MANES

Dutch- and French-braided tails for horses with long manes are very similar to hunter-braided tails. The difference is that these are braided only halfway down the tailbone with a very simple finishing braid.

YOU WILL NEED

Spray bottle or sponge
Comb
One 2-foot (60cm) length
  of yarn or string
Scissors

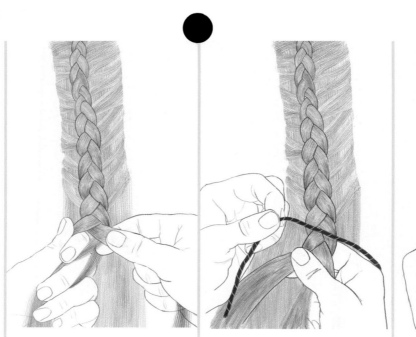

**DUTCH-BRAIDED
TAIL FOR HORSES
WITH LONG MANES**

1

2

3

PREP WORK
Start a Dutch braid as described on pages 30–32.

Continue adding hair from each side to the underside of the Dutch braid until you are about one-third of the way down the tailbone.

Use the bottom of the Dutch braid to start an underhanded three-strand braid. Lay a folded piece of yarn on top of the braid, then add it to the first and third sections of hair as described on page 34.

Continue braiding for several turns, then pinch the end of the braid with one hand while you use the other hand to separate one of the pieces of yarn from the hair.

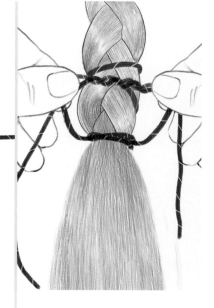

4

Make a loop with the yarn and rest the loose end on top of the braid at a right angle. Then pass the loose end behind the braid and through the loop.

5

Pull the yarn tight so that it creates a knot.

6

Repeat this process of looping and knotting the yarn from the other side of the braid, with the other end of yarn. Pull both ends of the yarn tight.

7

Tie a braiding square knot (see pages 36–37) around the base of the braid.

DUTCH-BRAIDED TAIL FOR HORSES WITH LONG MANES

8

Cut off the ends of the yarn, allowing the loose hairs to blend in with the remainder of the tail.

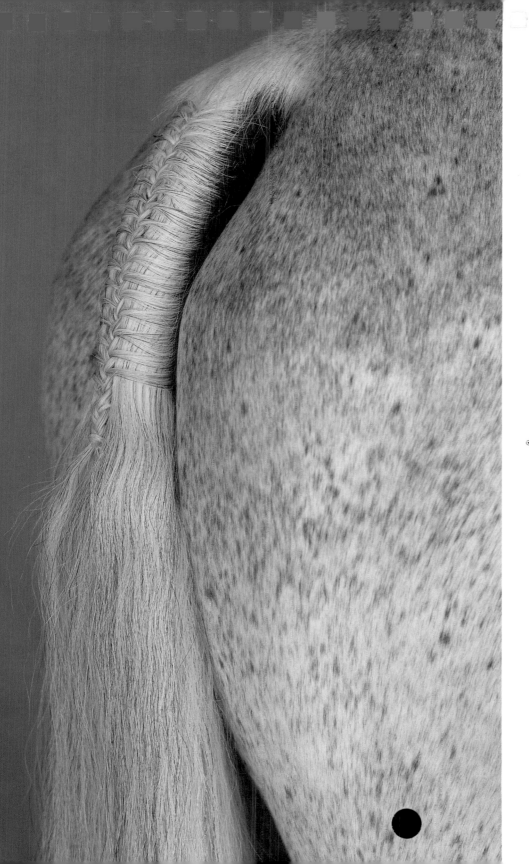

FRENCH-BRAIDED TAIL FOR HORSES WITH LONG MANES

Many dressage horses have the sides of the tail clipped short to accentuate the haunches. This braid gives the same effect without trimming the hairs.

YOU WILL NEED
Spray bottle or sponge *Comb* *One 2-foot (60 cm) length* *of yarn or string* *Scissors*

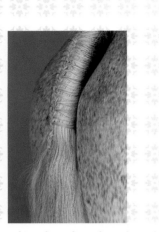

FRENCH-BRAIDED
TAIL FOR HORSES
WITH LONG MANES

PREP WORK
Start a French
braid as described
on pages 27–29.

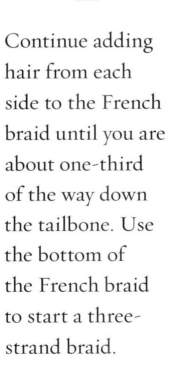

I

Continue adding
hair from each
side to the French
braid until you are
about one-third
of the way down
the tailbone. Use
the bottom of
the French braid
to start a three-
strand braid.

2

Insert a folded
piece of yarn as de-
scribed on page 34.
Continue braiding
for several turns,
then pinch the end
of the braid with
one hand while
you use the other
hand to separate
one of the pieces of
yarn from the hair.

3

Make a loop with
the yarn and rest
the loose end on
top of the braid at
a right angle. Then
pass the loose end
behind the braid
and through the
loop.

4

Pull the yarn tight
so that it creates
a knot.

5

Repeat this process
of looping and
knotting the yarn
from the other side
of the braid, with
the other end of
yarn. Pull both ends
of the yarn tight.

6

Tie a braiding
square knot (see
pages 36–37)
around the base of
the braid and cut
off the ends of the
yarn, allowing the
loose hairs of the
braid to blend in
with the remainder
of the tail.

WESTERN MANE BANDING

In Western pleasure and halter classes, grooming and presentation of the horse are as important as obedience and performance. Banding the horse's mane became popular in these classes in the mid-1980s as an aesthetic practice used to display a neat, balanced line on the horse's neck. In addition to improving the horse's general appearance, banding the mane can help a short neck appear to be longer and more attractive. This is done by increasing the number of small sections of mane that are used in the banding process.

The other function of mane banding is to keep the mane still while the horse is moving. Western pleasure horses are judged on the quality of their gaits. If the horses' mane is consistently still, instead of flopping with each step, their gaits will appear to be smooth. The forelock may also be banded; if it is not, it should be brushed so that it lies flat to complete the polished look for the show ring.

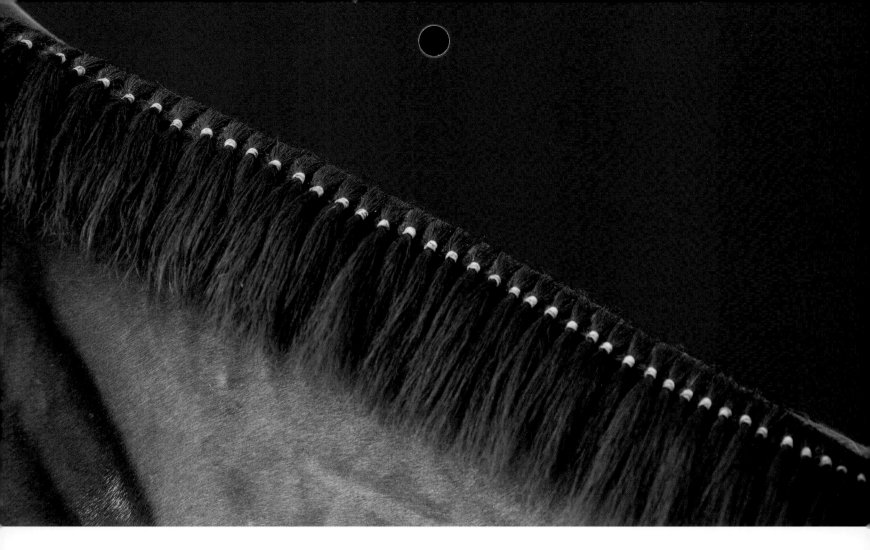

MANE AND FORELOCK BANDING

For some Western classes, such as halter, showmanship, pleasure, trail, horsemanship, and Western riding, banding the mane is a nice finishing touch that makes the neck look slimmer. It requires a well-prepared mane that is very evenly pulled. Commerical braiding rubber bands are available in a variety of colors to match different manes.

YOU WILL NEED
Stool
Spray bottle or sponge
Comb
Hair clip
Rubber bands

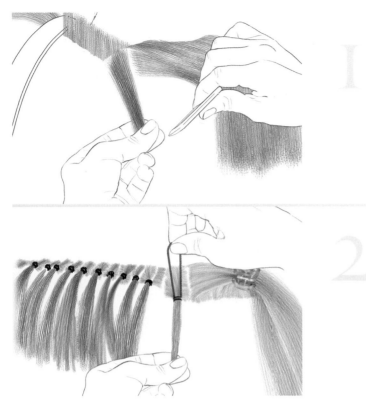

1 Start with a dampened, pulled mane. Use the comb to separate a portion of mane about ½ inch (1 cm) wide.

2 Use the hair clip to hold back the remainder of the mane. Wind a rubber band tightly around the separated lock of hair about 1 inch (3 cm) from the crest of the neck. If the bands are too close to the crest of the neck, the hair will stick out instead of lying flat. Repeat this process down the length of the neck, adjusting the rubber bands so that they are in a straight line.

SIMPLE
FORELOCK
BAND

TIPS FOR SUCCESS

🍀 *To visually lengthen a short neck, band smaller sections of hair; this will create more bands and make the neck look longer.*

🍀 *The forelock is not always banded; however, if you decide to band it, make sure that it lies flat.*

DRAFT HORSE BRAIDS

The tradition of braiding cloth into the mane may stem from the days when heavy horses were used for battle. A woman would give the knight her hair ribbon or scarf to wind into the horse's mane for good luck. In later years, when a hitch of horses was the only way to move merchandise, companies would try to outdo each other with impressively braided and decorated horses.

The mane roll and the tail bun are decorative braids that add a polished look to the draft horse in harness or in halter. Stallions and geldings are braided for halter classes but mares are generally shown unbraided.

Draft horses are braided with their manes hanging to the right side of the neck and the forelock generally pulled to the right ear. If the horse is in a hitch, however, the forelock can be pulled to the ear on the side of the hitch where the horse is harnessed so that the braid and colored ribbon will show.

MANE ROLL

Once the mane is braided, the horse will not be able to lower his neck, so keep him tied until you are ready to show. While rosettes are traditional and preferred, there is no regulation requiring them. You may also use commercially available silk flowers or ribbons that can be wired around the braid.

CROSSING COLORS

If using two colors, each piece of cloth (commercially available) or bunting should be 5 ½ feet (1.7 m) long and sewn together at one end so that the colors will alternate.

Tip for Success

Remember this basic sequence: Add a new section of hair, twist the two strands together, cross one side of the cloth over the intersection, then cross the other side over. Tighten the cloth.

Prep Work

Start with a combed mane.

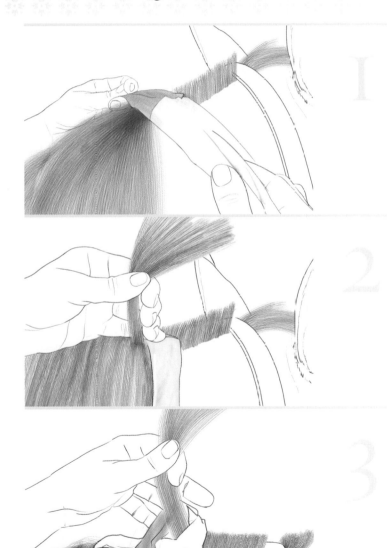

1 Lay the piece of cloth over the crest of the neck where the bridle path meets the mane so that it hangs at the same length on both sides.

2 From the top of the mane, near the crest, separate a section of hair about the same width as the piece of cloth.

3 Cross one side of the cloth around the section of hair and over to the other side of the horse. Do the same for the other side of the cloth.

MANE ROLL

4 Separate another section of hair from the crest of the neck.

5 Twist the two pieces of hair across each other, with the section closest to the ears crossing down under the other.

6 Cross the piece of cloth that is hanging on the side of the neck closest to you over and between the two sections of hair, and let the cloth hang over the opposite side of the neck, on the same side as the other end.

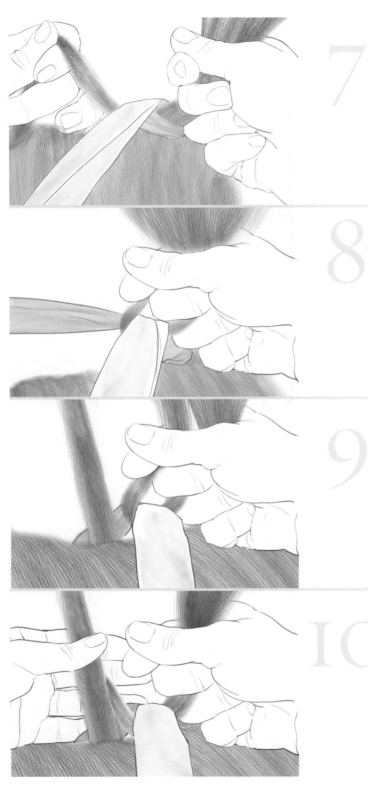

7 Cross the piece of cloth that was originally on the far side over the first piece, so it hangs over the side of the neck nearest you.

8 Hold both strands of hair in the hand closest to the horse's ears and pull each end of cloth so that the braid is tight against the crest of the neck.

9 Use the other hand to separate a new piece of hair from the crest of the neck.

10 Add this new strand of hair to the section of hair closest to it.

MANE ROLL

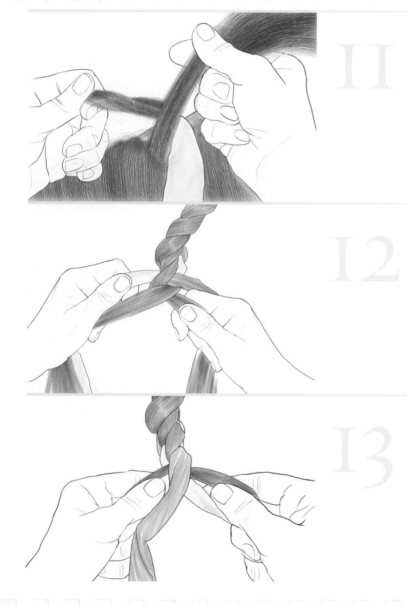

11 Twist the two strands together once, the same as with the initial sections of hair. Repeat steps 6–11, crossing the first end of the cloth under one section of hair and then over and between the two sections.

12 When you reach the area of the neck where the collar will rest, make a four-strand braid by twisting the two strands of hair together.

13 Cross the two pieces of cloth at a right angle against the two strands of hair.

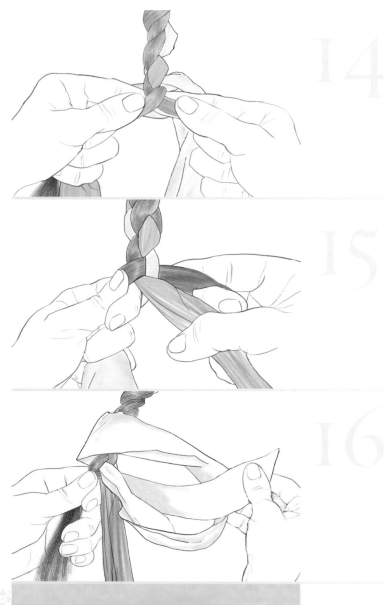

14 Twist the two strands of mane hair together again.

15 Cross the two pieces of cloth at a right angle against the two strands of hair again. Continue this braid for several turns.

16 Use one piece of cloth to tie a knot around the bottom of the braid, as if finishing with yarn (see page 34). Allow the remaining pieces of cloth to hang down.

FINISHING
Wire the first rosette at the top, the second one at the bottom, and the third one in the middle of the braid. Then space the two remaining rosettes evenly in between.

FOUR-STRAND FORELOCK BRAID

This four-strand braid is similar to the technique used to finish the mane roll, but it is done with ribbon instead of cloth.

YOU WILL NEED
Stool   *Rubber band*   *Two pieces of ribbon about 18 inches (46 cm) long and 1 inch (3 cm) wide*

MATCHING UP
The ribbon should be the same color as the cloth used for the mane roll.

TIP FOR SUCCESS

If your horse is in a hitch, you may want to braid the forelock to the outside so that it will show when the horses are hitched up.

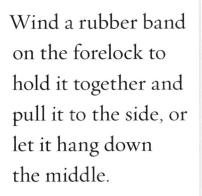

1	2	3	4

Wind a rubber band on the forelock to hold it together and pull it to the side, or let it hang down the middle.

Stack the two ribbons on top of each other, tie them together at the top, and then tie them in a loose knot similar to the first step of a braiding square knot.

Divide the forelock in half at the rubber band. Slip one strand of hair inside the loose knot and pull it tight.

Twist the two pieces of hair together once.

FOUR-STRAND
FORELOCK BRAID

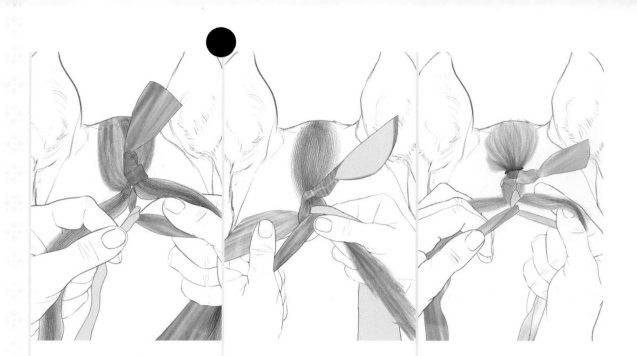

5

6

7

Cross the two pieces of ribbon at a right angle against the two strands of hair.

Twist the two strands of mane hair together again.

Cross the two pieces of ribbon at a right angle against the two strands of hair again. Continue making this four-strand braid for several turns.

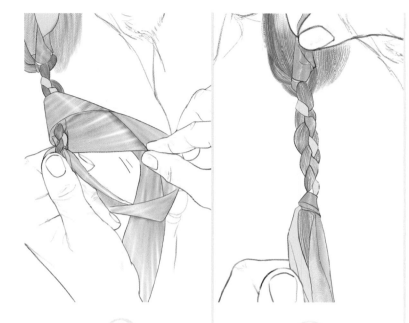

8

Use one of the
pieces of ribbon to
tie a knot around
the bottom of the
braid, as described
on page 34.

9

Allow the ends of
the ribbon to hang
down. Trim the
top and bottom of
the ribbons at an
angle to finish.

TAIL BUN

A neat tail bun with decorations that match the mane roll give a colorful balance and continuity to the draft horse that is ready for show.

YOU WILL NEED

Comb
Long shoelace that matches the color of your horse's tail hair
Elastic tail decoration to match the mane roll

TIP FOR SUCCESS

The middle section of hair from the bottom of the tail will be bigger than the two side sections, so as soon as you start braiding, borrow hair from the larger section and add it to the smaller sections until they are approximately the same width.

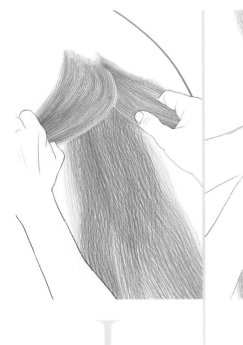

1

Separate two
sections of hair
from each side
of the top of the
tailbone.

2

Comb the hair in
the middle upward
as high as it will go
between the two
side sections.

3

Cross the two side
sections in front
of the combed-up
section.

4

Bring the combed-
up section down
on top of the two
crossed sections as
the middle section.
Start a three-strand
braid.

TAIL BUN

TIP FOR SUCCESS

In step 6, you can also use a pull-through at the top of the braid and place the loose ends of the shoelace through the loop, then pull the entire braid and shoelace through.

Braid as close to the bottom as possible. Finish with the shoelace as if finishing with yarn, as described on page 34.

Bend the braid under and push the loose end of the braid from the bottom, up through the base of the braid, between the braid and the tailbone. Pull the braid through as far as possible.

Use one hand to firmly hold the braid up. Use the other hand to grip the sides of the tail and slide down the tailbone, bringing all of the loose hairs down and in toward the base of the braid.

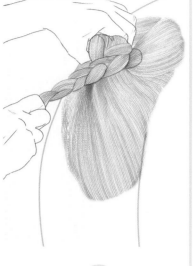

8

Keep holding the base of the braid, and with the other hand wrap the long part of the braid tightly around the bottom of the braid to form a bun. Continue wrapping the braid until all of the hair is wrapped around the base of the braid.

9

Twist the two ends of the shoelace together several times.

10

Separate the shoelace ends and wrap one over the top of the bun and the other under it. Tie a braiding square knot. Cut off the long ends, leaving a small amount on either side so that the knot does not come untied.

FINISHING WITH ROSETTES

Commercial tail decorations that attach with elastic are available to match the material used for the mane roll. Secure the elastic of the tail decoration around the bun.

SADDLEBRED & TENNESSEE
WALKING HORSE BRAIDS

Streaming back from the horse's mane and forelock, colorful ribbons add flair to complement the flashy gaits showcased in American Saddlebred and Tennessee Walker competitions. Both breeds were developed in the southern United States: the American Saddlebred became a recognized breed in 1891 and the Tennessee Walking Horse in 1935. Long before that, these breeds competed in shows, but exactly when the braiding tradition began is not clear. Possibly, by keeping the hair out of his ears, a forelock braid encouraged a horse to "use his ears" or prick them forward.

Tennessee Walking Horses are required to have braids in all English and halter classes. In contrast, for the American Saddlebred, braiding appears to be more of a tradition than a rule. The current rulebook specifies that Saddlebreds in the Country Pleasure Division cannot be braided. There is no requirement for braids in other divisions, yet they are routinely seen.

THREE-RIBBON FORELOCK BRAID

Braids for Saddlebreds and Tennessee Walking Horses are very similar, though Walking Horse braids are a few inches longer. The length of the mane braid is determined by the length of the forelock braid, so do the forelock braid first.

YOU WILL NEED

Helper
Stool
Three 32-inch-long (81 cm) lengths of 1-inch-wide (3 cm) ribbon
Scissors

TIP FOR SUCCESS

Your helper should hold the ribbons tightly, but not so tightly that they wrinkle.

Prep Work

Have your helper stand on the left side of the horse facing the left ear, with one hand on the halter. Stack the ribbons: dark, light, dark. Have your helper hold the ribbons on the horse's poll, with about 3 inches (8 cm) of ribbon sticking up above the poll.

1

Stand facing the horse's forehead and divide the forelock into three sections with a ribbon hanging down over each.

2

Wrap one ribbon around each section of hair, about 4 inches (10 cm) down the strand. This will create three wrapped pieces of hair.

3

Start a three-strand braid with the ribbon-wrapped hair. Keep braiding until you reach the nostrils.

4

Fold one of the darker ribbons over and tie a knot as described on page 34.

THREE-RIBBON
FORELOCK BRAID

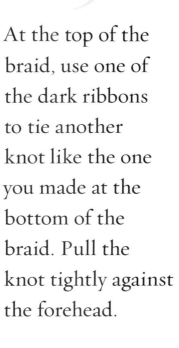

5

At the top of the braid, use one of the dark ribbons to tie another knot like the one you made at the bottom of the braid. Pull the knot tightly against the forehead.

6

To finish, cut the ends of the ribbons at the top and bottom of the braid in a V.

7

Pull the forelock braid to the side and slip it through the side of the halter so that it stays out of the horse's eyes and mouth.

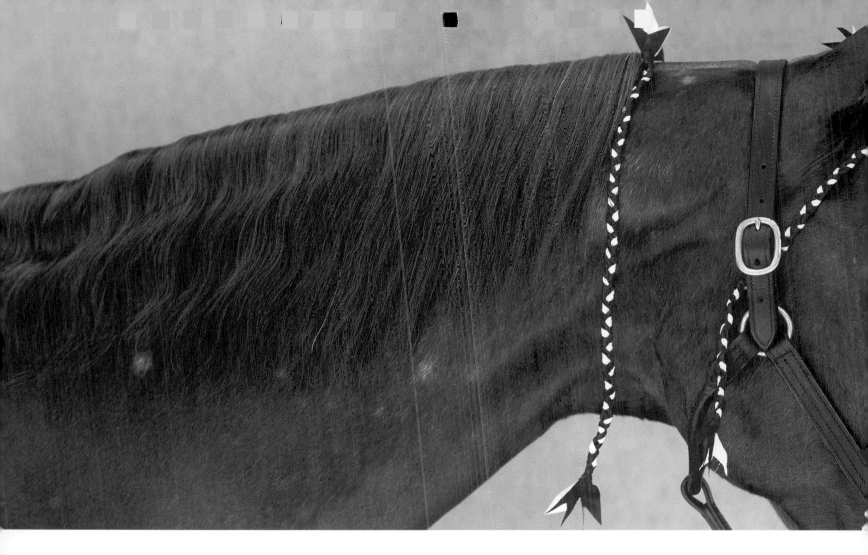

THREE-RIBBON
MANE BRAID

The mane braid needs to be slightly longer than the forelock braid when the horse's head is held high.

USING RIBBONS
It is customary to use two different colors of ribbon, usually one dark and one light, but one color can also be used. You will need a helper to hold the ribbons and to remind the horse to hold his head down.

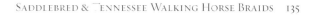

MANE THREE-RIBBON BRAID

PREP WORK

Separate a section of hair about ½ inch (1 cm) wide at the end of the bridle path. Stack and alternate three ribbons: dark, light, dark. Have your helper stand on the far side of the horse, with one hand on the halter. With three fingers of the other hand, she should hold back the remainder of the horse's mane, and with the thumb and forefinger she should hold the tops of the ribbon tightly about 3 inches (8 cm) above the crest of the neck.

1 With your helper holding the tops of the ribbons, divide the section of mane into two parts. These two parts will be the first and third sections of a three-strand braid.

2 Using the first and third pieces of ribbon, wrap the sections of hair. Allow the second ribbon to hang down as the middle section.

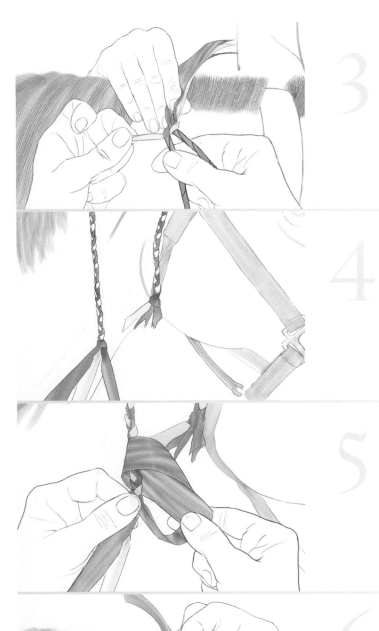

3 Start a three-strand braid with the two ribbon-wrapped strands and single piece of ribbon.

4 Continue braiding until the braid hangs past the jawline, so that it will be slightly longer than the forelock braid, when the horse's head is up, and the braid is tucked under the halter.

5 Fold one of the darker ribbons over and tie a knot as described in the section on finishing a braid with yarn on page 34.

6 At the top of the braid, use one of the darker ribbons to tie another knot. To finish, cut the ends of the ribbons in a V at both the top and bottom of the braid.

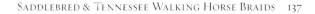

FUN BRAIDS

If you have mastered some of the more traditional braids, you can try other types that vary in complexity. Horse tails and manes are an excellent medium in which to practice and display this true art form.

The braids in this chapter are purely for the joy of braiding, but to keep the activity fun, it must also be safe. Always be careful and alert when working around horses, especially when you are climbing on stools and using sharp objects such as scissors. Most horses enjoy the attention that is inherent in being braided, but make sure that your horse's patience does not wane during a long session. It is also crucial that you keep enough space between you, your horse, and any solid object or wall so that if there is a problem, you always have an escape route.

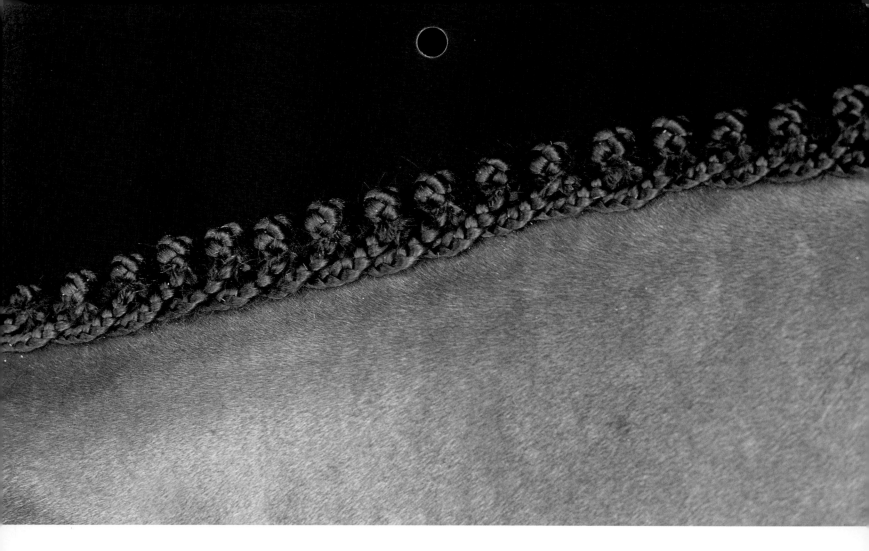

SCALLOPED BRAIDS

This braid requires a mane that is pulled to about 4 inches
(10 cm) long. This fashionable braid for English hunter horses
is not traditionally used due to its complexity; however, it can
add a special touch for a championship class.

YOU WILL NEED

Stool
Spray bottle or sponge
Pulling comb
30 2-foot (60 cm) lengths of
    yarn or string
Pull-through
Scissors

PREP WORK

Separate a section of pulled, dampened mane about 2½ inches (6 cm) wide. Complete a three-strand braid finished with yarn, as described on page 34. Complete three-strand braids for the entire mane.

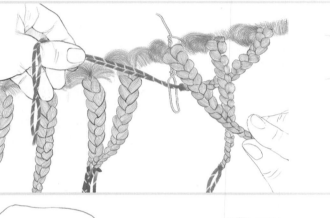

I Push the pull-through down through the third braid. Place the ends of the yarn from the first braid through the pull-through and pull them through the third braid, making sure the first braid lies flat against the neck.

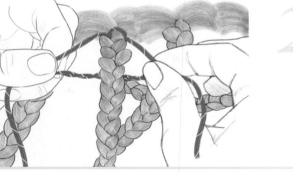

2 Separate the ends of the yarn and tie a braiding square knot, as described on pages 36–37, underneath the braid that you have pulled the ends of the yarn through.

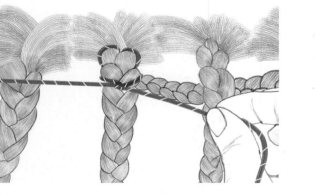

3 Then tie a braiding square knot in front, slightly below the crest of the neck. Pull the knot tight so that the braid is close to the neck, then cut off the tails of the yarn. Repeat steps 1–3 down the mane.

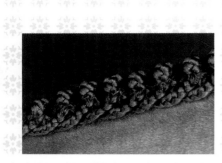

SCALLOPED BRAIDS

4 When you reach the last two braids, push the pull-through down through the last braid (this will be the second time that you are using the last braid, as the third-to-last braid is already tied to it).

5 Put ends of the yarn of the second-to-last braid through the loop in the pull-through and pull the ends of the yarn up through the top of the braid.

6 Tie a braiding square knot underneath the last braid. Tie a braiding square knot in front of the last braid, slightly below the crest of the neck, and pull the knot tight. Cut off the tails of the yarn, just as you did above.

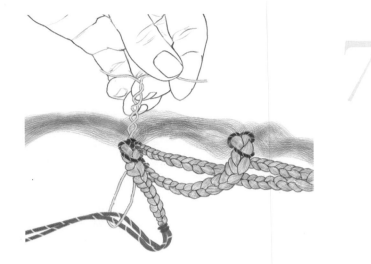

Push the pull-through down through the last braid for the third time, and put the ends of the yarn of that same braid through the loop of the pull-through. Pull the braid up through the top of the last braid, and tie off the loop just as you would loop for a hunter braid, as described on page 54.

FINISHING THE FORELOCK

The forelock can be braided as a simple or a French forelock, as described on pages 56–58.

FISHTAIL BRAID

The fishtail braid is not used for shows, but it is a fun braid for just showing off.

╔══════════════════════╗
║   **YOU WILL NEED**   ║
╚══════════════════════╝
Spray bottle or sponge
Comb
Rubber band

PREP WORK

Comb out and dampen the tail hairs, especially the ones at the top and sides of the tail.

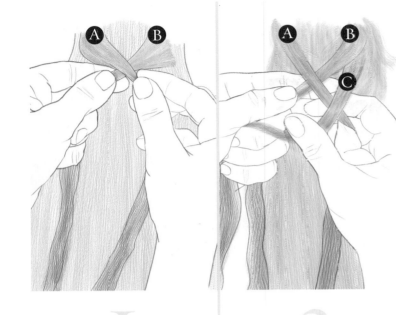

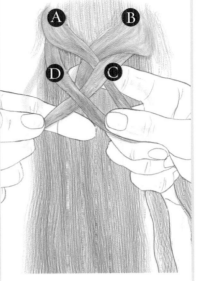

1

At the top of the tail, separate two small sections of hair from the left (A) and right (B) sides, then cross the left piece over the right.

2

Hold these pieces in your left hand. Separate another small section from the right side (C) of the tail, cross it over (A) and add it to (B).

3

Hold the two pieces in your right hand. Separate another small section (D) from the left side and add it to (A). Continue in this manner until you are about three-quarters of the way down the tailbone.

4

Pull a piece of hair from underneath the right side, pull it over the top of the braid, and add it to the section in your left hand. Continue braiding until you reach the end of the hair. Secure with a rubber band.

FOUR-STRAND SQUARE BRAID

This braid looks like a rope when it is finished. It is a challenging braid, so be sure that you are an expert at the three-strand braid before you give this one a try.

╒═══════ YOU WILL NEED ═══════╕

Comb
Rubber band

TIP FOR SUCCESS

Practice this braid with four different colored ribbons tied to the back of a chair before braiding your horse's tail.

Basic Weave Pattern

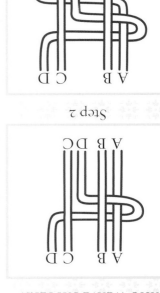

Step 2

Step 3

1

Divide the combed tail into four sections, with the two left sections in your left hand and the two right sections in your right hand.

2

Wrap the far right section D behind the tail to the left. Bring it forward over section A and weave it back under section B, ending between sections B and C.

3

Wrap section A behind the tail to the right. Bring it forward over section C, weave it under section D, then back between sections B and D.

Tip for Success

If you lose your place while braiding, always start with the section that is at the back of the braid. Move it under the braid to the opposite side and continue the pattern as described.

FOUR-STRAND
SQUARE BRAID

BASIC WEAVE PATTERN

Step 4

4

Beginning with section C on the far right, repeat step 2, moving right to left. Bring it over section B and under section A, so that it is between sections A and D.

5

Beginning with section B on the far left, repeat step 3, moving from left to right, then repeat step 2, moving from right to left. This is the basic pattern that is repeated to the end of the braid.

6

Continue alternating these steps until you have come to the end of the tail. When you reach the end of the hair, fasten the braid with a rubber band.

FOUR-STRAND WEAVE BRAID

The four-strand weave is a flat braid that is easy to master. It has a tendency to twist, which can add to its visual appeal.

YOU WILL NEED

Comb
Rubber band

ODD VS. EVEN

This braid can be done with five strands as well. An odd number of strands prevents the braid from twisting.

FOUR-STRAND WEAVE BRAID

BASIC WEAVE PATTERN

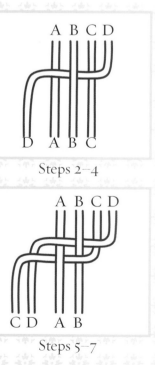

Steps 2–4

Steps 5–7

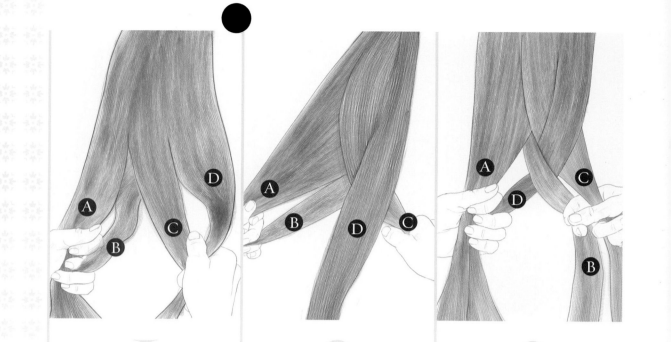

1

Divide the combed tail into four sections.

2

Weave section D over section C.

3

Weave section D under section B.

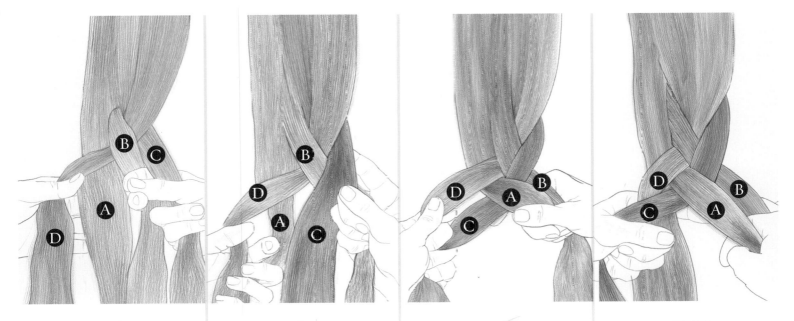

4

Weave section D over section A, so that it becomes the new far-left section.

5

Weave section C over section B.

6

Weave section C under section A. You always take the section from the far right and weave it over to the left.

7

Weave section C over section D, so that it becomes the new far-left section. Continue weaving the far-right sections from right to left until you reach the end. Fasten the braid with a rubber band.

*The mission of Storey Publishing is to serve our customers by
publishing practical information that encourages
personal independence in harmony with the environment.*

Edited by Deborah Burns and Sarah Guare

Cover and text design by Alethea Morrison
Text production and art direction of photography by
Jessica Armstrong
Illustrations by Melanie Powell

Front cover photograph by © Rachel Crowe/CORBIS
Back cover photographs by © Dusty Perin: top; and © Charles
Mann/www.cmannphoto.com: bottom

Interior photographs by © William Shepley, except for those
by © Mark J. Barrett/www.markjbarrett.com: 8; © Mat
Bastian: 130; © Sandra Lee Huston: 114; © Charles Mann/
www.cmannphoto.com: 68, © Charles Mann/www.arnd.nl:
76; © Dusty Perin: 7 top row, 2nd from left, 16, 22, 38, 110,
122, 124, 138; © Lesley Ward: 50

© 2007 by Charni Lewis

The information in this book is true and complete to the best of our
knowledge. All recommendations are made without guarantee on the part of the
author or Storey Publishing. The author and publisher disclaim any liability in
connection with the use of this information. For additional information please
contact Storey Publishing, 210 MASS MoCA Way, North Adams, MA 01247.

Storey books are available for special premium and promotional uses and for
customized editions. For further information, please call 1-800-793-9396.

Printed in China by R.R. Donnelley
10 9 8 7 6

LIBRARY OF CONGRESS CATALOGING-IN-PUBLICATION DATA

Lewis, Charni.
  Braiding manes and tails / Charni Lewis.
    p. cm.
  Includes index.
  ISBN 978-1-58017-699-6 (hardcover with concealed wire-o : alk. paper)
  1. Horses—Grooming. 2. Braid. I. Title.
SF285.7.L49 2008
636.1'0833—dc22

                                                              2007042265

ACKNOWLEDGMENTS

*For endless patience, all of the photography for illustrations, and tremendous moral and editorial support, I owe
an extreme debt of gratitude to my love, Rick Catt.*

*I also want to thank: Walt Lewis, Decker, Oliver, and the rest of my family for their continuous love, support,
and patience with lots of late nights. Andy Klug and Karla Skalsky for doing beautiful braids. Andres Diaz Zamora
and Catherine Berry for loads of hard work. Ambush, Ride, Irv, Roo, Red, Tucker, Quillan, Ferris, Ares, Café
Rojo, Kismet, Laredo, and all of their owners. Flintridge Riding Club for allowing us to take over the barn area
for a day. Doug Fog and Matt Anderson for teaching me about draft horse braids. Linda Hayes of Hazy Meadow
Ranch for supplying a draft horse and beautiful draft horse braids.*